Powerful Parent
Letters for K-3

CORWIN
PRESS

The Corwin Press logo—a raven striding across an open book—represents the happy union of courage and learning. We are a professional-level publisher of books and journals for K-12 educators, and we are committed to creating and providing resources that embody these qualities. Corwin's motto is "Success for All Learners."

Powerful Parent Letters for K-3

Mary Anne Duggan

CORWIN PRESS, INC.
A Sage Publications Company
Thousand Oaks, California

For information:

Corwin Press, Inc.
A Sage Publications Company
2455 Teller Road
Thousand Oaks, California 91320
E-mail: order@corwin.sagepub.com

SAGE Publications Ltd.
6 Bonhill Street
London EC2A 4PU
United Kingdom

SAGE Publications India Pvt. Ltd.
M-32 Market
Greater Kailash I
New Delhi 110 048 India

Printed in the United States of America

Library of Congress Cataloging-in-Publication Data

Duggan, Mary Anne.
  Powerful parent letters for K-3 / Mary Anne Duggan.
    p.   cm.
  Includes bibliographical references.
    ISBN 0-8039-6585-0 (cloth : acid-free paper). — ISBN
  0-8039-6586-9 (pbk. : acid-free paper)
    1. Schools—United States—Records and correspondence—Forms.
  2. Parent-teacher relationships—United States. 3. Early childhood
  education—Parent participation—United States. I. Title.
  LB2845.7.D85 1997
  372.119′2—dc21   97-4818

This book is printed on acid-free paper.

97 98 99 00 01 02 03 10 9 8 7 6 5 4 3 2 1

Corwin Press Production Editor: S. Marlene Head
Editorial Assistant: Kristen L. Green
Typesetter: Andrea D. Swanson
Cover Designer: Marcia R. Finlayson

Contents

Acknowledgments

I would like to thank first my own children's teachers throughout the years who delighted and enlightened me with their communications from school. Special thanks go to my daughter's current teacher and my fellow faculty member, Mary Kuopus, who writes the most professional and informative letters I've ever read. Three years ago, Mary shared a letter with our faculty explaining her spelling program, which planted the seeds for this book. Thank you also, Mary, for helping with the revision of this book's manuscript.

Many thanks go to my job share partner, Sally Peterson, who carried some of my load and tolerated having a partner caught in the frenzy of writing a book. Sally also read my letters and helped to make them what they are. I appreciate very much the support of my other teaching teammates, Wendy Beuerlein and Mary Zongolowicz, and thank them for all the wisdom they share with me daily.

My appreciation goes to my principal, Huck Fitterer, who has supported me in my job share situation for three years. I originally worked part-time to take care of my babies, and now that they are in school, this book has been my "baby." So I thank him for being supportive of both the mother and the writer in me.

I am grateful for the opportunity I was given to work with Ann McMartin and Corwin Press. Both Ann and Corwin enthusiastically embraced this project and have a real desire to put truly useful materials into the hands of teachers.

Most of all, thanks to my cheerleaders—my mother, June Peterson, and my husband, Sean. They never lost faith in me or this book, and I owe them a great debt for their patience and constant encouragement. Thanks especially go to my children, Taylor and Seanie, who enable me to have the dual perspective of parent and teacher and who give me joy beyond description.

About the Author

Mary Anne Duggan has taught children ages 3 through 13 for 11 years and is the former owner of a private preschool. She currently teaches kindergarten in Scottsdale, Arizona at Aztec Elementary School, a school known for its many innovations. As part of the faculty that opened Aztec Elementary four years ago, Duggan has been using integrated thematic instruction, multiage groupings, cooperative learning groups, brain-compatible learning, and other research-based educational practices. Duggan has a B.A. in elementary education and an M.Ed. in counselor education from Arizona State University. She keeps current on what works in the classroom by writing on educational and parenting topics. Her articles have appeared in *Learning, Grit,* and *Growing Parent* magazines, as well as several regional parenting publications. She resides in Scottsdale, Arizona with her husband, Sean, and two children, Taylor and Seanie.

Introduction

This book was born out of a real need my fellow kindergarten teachers and I have. We are using many teaching practices that are quite different from what our students' parents experienced when they were in school. Therefore, we spend an inordinate amount of our time explaining educational buzzwords such as integrated instruction, cooperative learning, multiple intelligences, and multiage groupings. So along with our teaching duties of planning, instructing, and assessing, we have to educate parents on effective classroom strategies with whatever time is left, which averages about 7.3 minutes a day. But how else can we expect parents to understand what we believe is best for children, unless we offer them the kind of information we receive through our continual professional development?

In addition, many of us are teaching in crowded classrooms with a large number of duties that lie beyond the scope of teaching children. We need all the help we can get, and parents can offer that help. I remember one day in particular, my colleagues and I were sitting around the faculty room discussing how our students were not taking responsibility for their backpacks and the papers that need to go home. "We need to write a letter to send home about encouraging self-reliance," one of us said. Each one of us nodded in consensus, but then a dead silence fell. We all wanted the letter to go home, but none of us had the time to sit down, compose, and design such a letter. Unfortunately, when we fail to engage parents, we actually make our jobs that much harder.

Powerful Parent Letters for K–3 offers teachers the timesaving advantage of having a year's worth of letters at their fingertips. This book saves teachers time by both educating parents about current educational practices and enlisting their help with problems teachers cannot tackle on their own. This book is primarily intended for teachers in K–3 classrooms of all kinds, although many of the letters can be used or adapted for use in preschool or intermediate grade classrooms. Principals can easily extract the information contained in the letters for use in a school newsletter or newspaper.

The content presented in *Powerful Parent Letters for K–3* can be used to guide face-to-face conversations with parents as well. For example, if you need to speak with Johnny's parents about problems that occur when he skips breakfast, read the letter titled "Sleep and Nutrition" first. What is contained in the letters is useful, research-based information that can be shared orally as well as through writing.

The book begins by jump-starting a teacher's written communication efforts. The first section, "Designing Your Own Powerful Parent Letters," offers "10 Steps to Effective Written Communication" and outlines the anatomy of a well-written letter. Tips are also given for how to organize a personal parent communication system.

The next section, "Ready-Made Letters," contains a wealth of letters grouped under the following headings:

- For Beginning the School Year
- On Classroom Practice
- On Curriculum
- For Building Home-School Partnerships
- On Parenting
- On Children's Social Skills
- On How Children Learn
- On Child Development

The ready-made letters can be simply signed and sent out as is, or the information in them can be changed to fit a particular situation if necessary.

The section "Creating Letters for Behavioral Concerns" is divided into two categories:

- On Student Disrespect
- On Student Physical Violence

These letters need to be personalized, as they deal with topics that are more individual in nature. It's hard to find the right words sometimes when a child has been swearing or destroying property in the classroom. This section offers a format for writing such a letter to an individual student's parent, with helpful words and phrasings particular to each problem.

The last section contains other ready-to-use communication forms, and its purpose is to make a teacher's life easier. Broken down into reminders, reports, requests, and surveys, these forms allow a teacher to grab a form and fill in information quickly by inserting just a couple of words.

Finally, the book provides a broad overview for teachers who are seeking to use the most effective teaching methods possible. Just reading through the book is an exercise in professional development. It may confirm for teachers what they are already doing in the classroom or motivate them to investigate a topic further. One thing is for sure—using these letters will free up a teacher's time for things like professional development, or maybe even a personal life.

PART I

Designing Your Own Powerful Parent Letters

No matter how good your intentions, or how dedicated and hard-working you are as a teacher, your efforts may remain unnoticed and unsupported by parents. This may lead to feeling isolated and like "you have to do all the work yourself." But unless you tell parents what you plan—and thereby involve them in your classroom activities and in their children's learning at home—they will not know what is going on and will be unlikely to help you. One of the most efficient ways to reach and teach parents is by writing letters home that the student delivers. Well-written and informative letters to parents about classroom activities and their children's progress and development are essential if you are to get the maximum mileage from your efforts as a teacher.

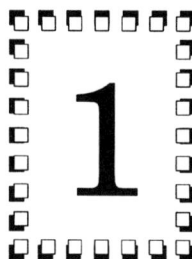

Getting Results From Your Communications

Writing a letter that gets results is an art form not taught in teacher preparation courses. Yet the power of written communication justifies the time spent on perfecting this art. Headaches associated with writing letters to parents can be eliminated by learning tips for writing effective letters, pitfalls to avoid, and how to organize your parent communication system. Other forms of communication with parents, such as by phone or by e-mail, can be powerful, too, and follow many of the same rules of written communication.

10 Steps to Effective Written Communication

1. Communicate with regularity. When parents receive regular written communication from their child's teacher, they are more likely to take the communication seriously. Parents get into a routine of sitting down, perhaps weekly, and reading a note from their child's teacher. By sending out regular forms of communication, you are presenting yourself as a caring professional.

2. Use correct spelling and grammar. Your letter might dazzle with information, but one grammatical error can take away from the competent image you are trying to convey. The importance of proper English usage in communication with parents cannot be underestimated. If at all possible, ask another adult to proofread all communications before they are sent home.

3. Consider your audience. Consider the reading level and sophistication of your parent community. This will determine whether you write lengthy letters or shorter ones, perhaps written in list format. All teachers, however, should be careful not to condescend. It's easy to do after working with young children all day. When writing a letter, take a moment to shift out of "kid mode" and gear your letter to a fellow adult.

4. Stay positive. Your written communications will make a lasting impression. They may be read over and over, and parents will glean a lot about who you are from what they read. Another practice to avoid is writing when you are angry. If Janie bit three other students today, don't write the letter while the teeth marks are still fresh. Take time to compose a calm, rational letter. You'll be glad you did.

5. Be direct. If you need wrapping paper rolls by Tuesday or parents to come on the field trip to a museum or a dairy farm, state it clearly near the top of your letter. Set apart important information in a list format to ensure the best result.

6. Always make and keep a copy. Letters on behavioral concerns tend to get lost. Having an extra copy on hand helps when you need to send home a duplicate (this time with a phone call beforehand). Also, duplicates can be worth their weight in copy paper when you need documentation on a growing behavior problem.

7. Keep it brief. Parents today are busy, if nothing else. They will know you understand their plight by sending home letters that don't chip away at what little time they have to relax and be with their families.

8. Use humor when appropriate. Humor can build a bridge between you and your students' parents. It helps to reduce some of the seriousness involved with raising and educating young children. Humor makes you more approachable as a teacher.

9. Communicate partnership. Convey in all your communications that you and your students' parents are working in concert for the good of the children. Emphasize that education is triangular, with the student, parents, and teacher all working together to promote the child's success.

10. Don't hide behind a letter. Nothing replaces face-to-face communication. Letters are time effective because they reach a large group of people with a small amount of time invested, or they address subjects that don't require an in-person meeting at the moment. Sometimes letter writing can be a way of avoiding conflict that might arise when communicating with parents. In cases where a personal conference is needed, a letter may serve to make the situation worse.

Organizing Your Parent Communication System

Communicating through writing is made easier with these organizational tips:

Make a calendar. Design a plan of when you will send out letters, and mark the dates on a calendar. Check off the dates when the letters are sent out, so you know what you've sent out and when you sent it. The need for some letters will just arise, as when students are having difficulty saying goodbye in the morning (see the letter "Separation Anxiety") or if you have a child with special needs who is new to the class (see the letter "Inclusion of Students With Special Needs"). Decide what you want parents to know about your classroom this year, and send home a weekly letter explaining the practice. Examples of letters to include in this parent education program are "Cooperative Learning," "Multiage Groupings," "Constructing Knowledge," and "Learning Through Play."

Vary the format. Color coding your letters makes finding and grouping them easier for you and increases the chances your letter will be read by parents. For example, printing all classroom newsletters on pink paper directs the parent to recognize it as such, which differentiates newsletters from other "junk mail" parents receive from school. Writing individual letters on a consistent color directs parents' attention to the personal nature of the letter. When sending out the letter "Choosing Clothes" from the parenting section, printing it on blue paper, for example, will remind parents of the last blue letter you sent on "Chores." The parents will see the logic in your communications and the efforts you are making to share useful information.

Use take-home folders. Either purchase with school money or ask parents to provide a folder at the beginning of the year that will be used to transport communications back and forth. Paper folders will not last long, unless laminated. Plastic folders with pockets are best. Place the child's name and room number on the folder in case it gets lost. Have a specific place where students put their take-home folders when they enter the room, and ask them to unpack their folders and put any papers from home in a consistent place. At the end of the day, save ample time for packing up folders.

Keep a communication folder for each child. For all those "please sign and return" forms, keep an individual folder for each child where you place the signed forms. In addition, when sending out a letter to an individual parent, always place a copy of the letter in this file for your records. Keep notes of any phone conversations you have with parents. The trick is to amass all written and verbal communications in case it comes to the point where documentation of parent contact is needed.

Make a check sheet. Make two class lists side by side on an 8-½-by-11-inch piece of paper, with a small, horizontal line for placing checkmarks next to each student's name. Copy and cut the paper in half vertically, so one list is on each side. This makes for a handy checklist when you need to see who has returned a communication that was sent to the whole class, such as a permission slip. Keep one checklist taped to your desk at all times. When you send an individual letter home that needs to be signed and returned, write the date next to that child's name on the checklist. When the letter is returned, simply cross off the date. Staple the returned portion with the parent's signature to your copy of the letter. Remember to look at the checklist each morning to see if any letters or forms are due back to you.

Classify your letters. Certain letters will be used at specific times of the year, such as "How to Help in the Classroom" at the start of the school year and "Boredom" toward the end. Copy the letters along with any others you have written, and file them according to the month they will be used. Check the folder at the end of each month to see what next month's letters will be.

Anatomy of an Effective Letter

Most often, a teacher writes an individual letter to a student's parents because there is some problem occurring with the student in the classroom. One goal of the communication is to inform parents about the problem, and another goal is to elicit their help. By following a format for writing this type of letter, all the important information is sure to be included. (The letters in the section "Creating Letters for Behavioral Concerns" all follow this format.)

Section 1: Letterhead, Date, and Greeting

Use school letterhead, or place your name, school address, and school phone number at the top center of the page. If a parent needs to call you back, it is helpful to have the school phone number right on the letter. Always date the letter and use "Dear" in your greeting. Whether you address the parent by first or last name is up to you. But keep the form consistent with how you sign your letter. (For example, "Dear Mr. Green" and "Sincerely, Mrs. Jones.")

Section 2: The Body

In the first paragraph, identify the problem as specifically as possible. Use the five Ws—who, what, where, when, and why. In the second paragraph, tell what interventions have been tried so far and give suggestions for how the parent can help. Be concrete ("When Jaime looks like he's going to throw something, remind him with a code word to stop and count to 10.") Give two or three suggestions. In the third paragraph, wrap up the letter by offering assurance. Communicate that you and the child's parents will be working together to help the child. Often, a letter home packs a punch for parents, and a few reassuring, kind words can soften the blow.

Section 3: The Closing

Sign the letter with "Sincerely" or "Yours truly." Always include a space for the parent to sign and return the bottom portion of the letter.

Format for an Effective Letter

Place school or personal letterhead here
(with name, address, city/state/zip, and phone number)

Date

Dear (parent's name):

First paragraph: Identify the problem. State who, what, where, when, and why. Following are some possible leads:

"I have noticed . . . "
"I am working with Julie on . . . "
"I wanted you to know about . . . "

Second paragraph: Explain what has been done so far about the problem. Offer suggestions for possible home interventions. Be specific and give two or three ideas. Following are some possible leads:

"Some suggestions to help with this problem are . . . "
"We are going to try . . . "
"I recommend . . . "

Third paragraph: Wrap it up by offering reassurance. Convey here that teacher and parents are partners in helping the child. Following are some possible leads:

"Together we should be able to help . . . "
"I will keep working with . . . "
"Thank you for your time and continued support."

Sincerely,

Sample Effective Letter

Mary Anne Duggan
Aztec Elementary School
13636 N. 100th Street
Scottsdale, AZ 85260
(602) 451-5080 ext. 5203

November 4, 1997

Dear Mr. and Mrs. James:

I am writing because Lisa was aggressive with the other children today. She pulled another student's hair in the lunch line, and she poked the child sitting next to her with a pencil during art class. Also, Lisa kicked over the block building some other students were working on during centers.

When I asked Lisa about the cause of these behaviors, a theme emerged. She said the students were not listening to her and, in the case of the blocks, would not let her play. On each occasion, I spoke with Lisa about the choices she could have made. Lisa needs help with learning how to get the attention of other students in appropriate ways. I recommend that we both reinforce Lisa's behavior when we see her joining a group or eliciting attention in acceptable ways. If Lisa behaves aggressively, I suggest we role-play workable ways for gaining attention.

If we watch Lisa closely over the next couple of weeks and intervene when she needs help, I think she will learn these skills quickly. Thank you for your time and continued support, and please call me if you have any further questions.

Sincerely,

Mary Anne Duggan

- -

Please sign and return this portion of the letter by 11/5/97.

X_____
     Signature   Date

Other Forms of Communication

Letters and notes home are only one piece of the parent-communication pie. Other forms may be more efficient and effective, depending on the circumstance.

Use the telephone. Call parents about any problem of a severe nature. As with written communications, be sure you're cool before calling. Survey parents at the beginning of the year to determine the best time to call them and if they can receive nonemergency calls at work. (See Letter 2.2: "Classroom Communication.") The information contained in this book can be used to frame your phone conversations. Highlight key phrases before dialing to make the most of your phone conference.

Send an e-mail. If you have access to e-mail, put technology on your side to contact parents efficiently. You will save a lot of paper by sending messages to parents electronically. Again, survey parents to create an e-mail address book. Avoid an e-mail faux pas by always double-checking the address of the person to whom you are sending an e-mail. Also, direct parents in your messages to send an e-mail message back to you to confirm they have received your message.

Create a web page. Dazzle your students' parents with an electronic newsletter. Designing your own web page is now easier than ever. Many school districts are presenting workshops on just how to do this, and on-line companies also offer assistance with this valuable communication tool. You can communicate as many pages of information as you want with this form of communication, without any trees paying the price for it.

PART
II

Ready-Made Letters

By simply adding a signature, ready-made letters can be sent home as is to address a variety of topics with parents. They also can serve as a guideline for any face-to-face conversations you may have with parents. Ready-made letters offer handy information at your fingertips, whatever the form of communication. The contents of the letters can also be extracted and placed in your classroom or school newsletter.

For Beginning
the School Year

At the start of the school year, parents have a certain amount of excitement peppered with anxiety about who you are and what you have to offer their child. One way to allay their fears is to communicate often from the beginning of the school year. The letters contained in this section will help you introduce yourself to your students' parents and start your year with their children on a positive note.

Rationale for
Sending Home These Letters

Back-to-School Letter. Many principals require teachers to send home basic information during the first week of school. Use this form to communicate supplies needed for the year, how and when parents can contact you, and your behavior guidance plan and to convey your warmth and professionalism.

Classroom Communication Letter. Not only does this letter elicit information from parents on how best to reach them by phone or e-mail, it is a call for open communication between parents and teacher. A request is made for parents to speak with the teacher first when concerns arise.

Homework Letter. Parents and teachers can have differing ideas on the specifics of homework—when, how much, how often. Parental complaints about amounts of homework often stem from difficulties parents and students are having with successfully completing homework. By laying out your homework plan and its philosophy, and by giving parents tips for helping their child, you will avert some of those homework concerns that can crop up at the beginning of the year.

How to Help in the Classroom Letter. Most parents need some instruction so that they can become good classroom helpers. This letter lists strategies for parents to follow. Some of them seem obvious, but it's best not to assume anything when asking adults to work with children.

Positive Guidance Letter. This letter informs parents how you encourage acceptable classroom behavior and handle misbehaviors when they occur. The letter lists your specific positive classroom management strategies and techniques and asks parents to support your program at home.

Separation Anxiety Letter. When separation problems arise, you need parents on your side. There are steps to help reduce anxiety, and they are listed in this letter. Even if you don't have students clinging to their parents' knees, send the letter anyway. Separation anxiety isn't always obvious, and many more families might benefit from this letter than you may think.

Letter 2.1

Back-to-School

Dear Parents:

Welcome to the new school year. I am looking forward to getting to know you and your child over the next few weeks. The start of the school year is such a special time, filled with anticipation and hopes of what the new year will bring. I'm sure you have many questions about how the classroom will be run and what will be expected of your child. I assure you I will be available to answer all of your questions. The best way to reach me is by calling _____ between the hours of _____. I will return your call on the same day. I believe our communication is vital to your child's success.

I am dedicated to helping your child develop cognitively, socially, physically, and emotionally. Our classroom will have a safe atmosphere where your child will take risks and experience success on a daily basis. Creating a solid foundation for future school success requires not only instruction in basic skills but also fostering a true love of learning in each child. Great efforts will be made each day to stimulate your child's naturally curious mind.

Your child will need some special supplies to start the school year. These supplies are:

If possible, please send these items to school with your child by _____. If you have any difficulty getting any of these supplies, please call me and I will help you obtain them.

Our class has a set of procedures that will provide a solid structure for how it operates. These procedures will be followed consistently to help your child navigate his or her way through the day. High behavioral expectations will be communicated to the students. We have a few classroom rules, and they are:

All matters of guidance will be handled with respect for all parties involved. One definition of guidance is "to influence." My objective with classroom guidance is to influence your child to be a happy, contributing member in the classroom.

I look forward to the many happy days your child and I will share. Thank you for your time.

Sincerely,

Classroom Communication

Dear _____,

Your child's success this year is dependent upon parent, student, and teacher working together as a team. It is vital that we keep the lines of communication open in both directions. This year, you will receive written updates on classroom happenings. In addition, if your child is having any difficulties, I will contact you by letter, phone, or e-mail. To reach you efficiently, I need the following information:

A phone number where you can be reached during school hours:

_____ home _____ work _____
                    (check one)

A phone number where you can be reached after school hours:

_____ home _____ work _____ between the hours of _____
                    (check one)

Can you be contacted at work for nonemergency calls? yes _____ no _____

E-mail address (if applicable): _____

How frequently do you check your e-mail? _____

In turn, please feel free to call me to discuss any questions, comments, or concerns you might have during the school year. As I will speak with you directly if I have any concerns about your child's school performance, please speak to me directly about any concerns you might have about your child's school experience. Many misunderstandings can be avoided if we speak with each other first whenever questions arise.

Please return this completed form to me tomorrow. Thank you for your time and for being an active participant in your child's education.

Sincerely,

Homework

Dear Parents:

Homework in the early years has its own character. It should be fun, open ended, and relate to the students' interests. One goal of homework in our classroom is to teach responsibility. Homework is also designed to build a bridge between home and school and to reinforce concepts learned at school. It teaches a child to use time wisely and helps improve memory. What I will do to meet these goals is as follows:

- Assign age-appropriate activities that are designed to practice skills and concepts already taught in class
- Make homework joyous
- Make homework student led
- Communicate the importance of homework

You can be supportive with homework by:

- Communicating a positive attitude toward homework
- Helping your child understand directions
- Encouraging your child to persevere through tough spots
- Suggesting your child call a classmate with homework questions
- Reviewing completed homework with your child, making suggestions (but not correcting it yourself)
- Writing a note if your child has extreme difficulty completing an assignment

Parents who are overinvolved with homework communicate to the child that he or she is not capable. A hands-off approach will leave some children frustrated and in despair. In addition, power struggles can occur between parent and child over homework. If this happens to you, ask someone else, your spouse or a sibling, to step in. Homework help can be perceived as criticism, and focusing on the positive before offering suggestions can help avoid this problem.

Successful studiers have certain things in common. They have a set time each day for homework to be completed. (This averts procrastination.) They work in proper lighting using at least a 100-watt bulb, with a large work surface in an area that is free from household distractions. Successful studiers take short breaks when necessary. They have materials at their fingertips and may even have a homework box to put in all incoming and outgoing homework and materials. They finish projects early.

With your guidance, your child can see homework as enjoyable and worthwhile, laying a solid foundation for later school years.

Sincerely,

How to Help in the Classroom

Dear Volunteer:

Thank you for offering to help out in your child's room. Our classroom is a richer place when volunteers share their many talents with our students. Working with children can be joyous, especially when these practices are used:

Learn and use the children's names. Using a child's name helps you seem more familiar to the child, and in turn the child will respond more positively.

Work with all children, not just your child. Often children like to cling to mom and dad when they come in to help. Encourage your child to "share" you. The more you come in, the less clingy your child will be.

Communicate in a positive way. Instead of saying, "Don't poke Billy," try "Please keep your hands to yourself." This increases the chance of the child following your request.

When looking at the children's artwork, take time to notice something unusual. Notice the way the child incorporated heart shapes in the drawing, or how the cowboy in the picture is wearing spurs. This is more sincere than "That's beautiful, Betsy!"

Keep in mind that all children develop at different rates. One child may struggle with reading but may be able to recite every species of dinosaur. We all have stronger and weaker areas. Acknowledge strengths when you see them.

Use only appropriate physical touch. If a child won't come to the group when you ask, speak to me about it rather than leading the child by the arm to the group. Children also have varying sensitivity levels to touch. Keep this in mind before you offer a pat on the back or a handshake.

Respect confidentiality. Feel free to talk to others outside of our room about activities and practices used in our classroom. Please keep individual students' names out of these conversations. If you would like to speak with me about a student, please choose a time when no students are within earshot.

Please call if you are unable to come in on your assigned volunteer day. Plans are made for ways you can help, so please let me know at your earliest convenience if you will be unable to help out on your day.

Relax and enjoy. Sharing your caring and enthusiasm is the best thing you can do for our classroom. Thank you for being an active partner in your child's education. Your child will never forget how you gave of yourself this year in our classroom.

Sincerely,

Positive Guidance

Dear Parents:

The primary goal of young children is to belong. When that need is not met, misbehaviors can occur in the classroom. Our classroom uses a system of positive guidance to deal with behavior in the classroom. The cornerstone of positive guidance is mutual respect, which is modeled and reinforced each school day. It is also based on the belief that children can learn to choose appropriate behaviors and can internalize the reasons for behaving appropriately.

To create a positive classroom climate, I will do the following:

- Take time to teach expected behaviors
- Explain rules in terms of how they benefit children
- Be consistent
- React to misbehaviors in a kind but firm manner
- Conduct problem-solving class meetings
- Phrase directions positively ("Please walk in the halls" instead of "No running!")
- Keep children busy with learning activities that are age appropriate
- Have well-defined classroom procedures
- Encourage children to use their words instead of fists to solve problems
- Have the class slogan "Never hurt anyone on the outside or the inside"

As a parent, please use the strategies that apply with your child at home. Another way you can help is to make sure your child is eating a well-balanced diet and is getting adequate sleep. Deficits in this area can create behavior problems. Finally, notify me if there is a change in your family structure, or if any other situation in your child's life may be affecting your child in school.

Misbehavior is actually "mistaken behavior," in that a child is confused as to how to belong. The focus, then, is to help that child learn how to get his or her needs met in appropriate ways. In our classroom, mistakes are viewed as opportunities to learn. Outcomes that are natural or logical for a behavior will be used. For example, if a child writes on a table, he or she will be asked to sponge off the writing. At times, a child will be removed from a troublesome situation, which is known as time-away. Time-away works when it is seen as a break for the child, until he or she can try again. The attention is paid to the behavior, not the child as a person.

With mutual respect, consistency, and a positive approach to guiding behavior, your child will learn to behave appropriately, and not just when an adult is looking.

Thank you in advance for your support, and remember, I am a phone call away if you have any questions, comments, or concerns.

Sincerely,

Letter 2.6

Separation Anxiety

Dear Parents:

Congratulations! You and your child have both survived the first few days of school. Your good-byes may be going smoothly now, or you may have a little one still tugging at your shirt as you exchange farewells. Separation anxiety at the beginning of the school year is common and with a little planning and forethought can be wiped away.

Some tips for saying good-bye are as follows:

- Put your child in charge of some part of the morning routine (dressing, packing the backpack). This will give your child a sense of control in the morning.
- Plan how you will say good-bye beforehand. Also, talk about what you will do when your child gets home.
- When you are saying good-bye, calmly communicate through your words and body language that you are confident your child will be okay. Make your good-bye brief. Lingering only increases the pain.
- Speak positively about school when at home with your child. If you are experiencing any anxiety, do not let your child sense it.
- Reinforce the connection between home and school. Have your child loan books to the class, bring a snack, or make something for a friend.
- If separation continues to be a problem, send a toy, object, or photograph with your child to help make separation easier.

Keep in mind that very few children keep up the tears after mom or dad has left the building. Children are wonderfully distractible and can usually be redirected into some interesting task. Rest assured that I will call you if your child is not settling down soon after you have left.

When we look at what the child may be anxious about, we can understand some of that fear. Imagine being dropped off at a party where you don't know anyone, you're not quite sure where the bathroom is, and the leader of the party is twice your size! At this party you are asked to stay many hours and socialize with complete strangers. Sometimes we expect social skills from children that we wouldn't expect from an adult.

Thankfully, separation anxiety does fizzle out, and soon those tugging-at-your-shirt-and-heart days will be a distant memory.

Sincerely,

On Classroom Practice

The more parents know about how your classroom operates, the more supportive they can be. Sending home letters on classroom practice is a way of pulling parents into the world of your classroom. They also help to instill confidence as you share your expertise with parents. Most important, they invite cooperation from parents, which is what every teacher really needs.

Rationale for
Sending Home These Letters

Active Listening Letter. Active listening is a critical skill for school and personal success. It is one skill that parents can easily support at home. This letter shows parents the steps of teaching active listening and gives tips for how to help their child listen more actively.

Assessing Student Progress Letter. Assessment is not what it used to be when our students' parents were young. Parents need to be shown the benefits of authentic assessment over traditional grading practices, which this letter outlines.

Book Orders Letter. This timesaving letter will help kick off your book-ordering procedures for the year. The letter is organized to streamline the book-ordering process.

Centers Letter. Centers time can be misunderstood, or regarded as purely "playtime." This letter tells of the intellectual and social gains children make during centers time.

Classroom Procedures Letter. This letter is for teachers who use the concept of procedures to help students negotiate their way through the day. Suggestions for using procedures at home are given.

Cooperative Learning Letter. Another misunderstood concept, cooperative learning has many merits, which are listed in this letter. This letter serves to discount myths about cooperative learning many parents have learned through the media and other sources.

How Children Are Grouped Letter. When parents ask, "Is my child in the high group?" you may want to pass out this letter. Research solidly supports heterogeneous grouping, and this letter explains to parents why mixed-ability groups work.

Inclusion of Students With Special Needs Letter. If you have a child or children with special needs in your class, send out this letter. People fear what they don't understand, and this idea applies to parents and inclusion. A little information will go a long way toward making your inclusion program work.

Multiage Groupings Letter. This foreign concept needs explaining to parents. Parents of older children in multiage classes fear their children will not be challenged. Parents of younger children are afraid their children might be negatively influenced by older kids. Multiage classes actually offer intellectual and social growth for all children, and this letter explains how.

Letter 3.1

Active Listening

Dear Parents:

"Okay, class, active listening, please." When my students hear this request, several behaviors can be observed. Their bodies and eyes turn toward me, they put down whatever might be in their hands, and they are not talking. As a class, we have decided specifically what active listening looks like, and in doing so the students have a model to go by when active listening is called for. Here are the behaviors my students use when actively listening:

- The listener's body and hands are still.
- The listener is looking at the speaker.
- The listener is not talking or making any other noises.
- Perhaps the listener is showing understanding by nodding his or her head.
- The listener is not interrupting the speaker.
- The listener is thinking about what is being said.
- The listener may ask a question or contribute when appropriate.

Active listening often does not develop naturally, and so breaking the skill into specific, observable parts can be helpful. You may want to role-play with your child what active listening looks like. Another way to teach active listening is to consistently model it yourself. Adults have been known to speak to children while working on something else, while muttering "That's nice, dear," which leaves the child feeling unheard. You may know some adults who could use "Active Listening 101." To listen actively is a learned skill and is crucial for your child's success in school and social relationships. It may be one of the most important skills we both work on with your child this year.

The Chinese believe that to actively listen, one must use the eyes, ears, heart, and self and give undivided attention. Listening is a complex skill people the world over are constantly refining.

Sincerely,

Assessing Student Progress

Dear Parents:

It would be nice if we could look through a window into a child's mind. Since we can't, teachers try many approaches to figure out what a student knows and doesn't know, what that student's strengths are, and where he or she might need help. This process is called assessment.

Assessment used to be thought of as grading. Grading is an easy, fast way to communicate student progress. But grades are nonspecific at best, and can be damaging at worst. Grades motivate children from the outside (extrinsically). In addition, traditional grading is done *to* children, denying them the opportunity to truly learn from the process of assessment.

This year, your child will play an active role in his or her assessment by helping to create a classroom portfolio. A portfolio consists of samples of work your child has completed across a variety of subject areas. Each paper is dated to demonstrate growth over time. Your child will discuss with me which items to include and which to leave out, and as a result your child will learn more about the learning process itself. Self-assessment leads to better performance.

Portfolios are far superior to grades alone in the amount of information they yield. By looking at a portfolio, you might see the evolution of your child's use of periods at the ends of sentences—not much in September, sprinkled here and there in October, and used consistently in November. You might see all the math skills your child has mastered by looking at completed work. Possibly, it will be clear that your child needs help writing the letter *b*. All this information and more is furnished in a portfolio. Parents whose children have portfolios learn much more about their child's progress than parents who hear their child earned a B in writing.

I will be adding other forms of assessment to the portfolio. I will observe your child working and will conduct individual conferences with your child. I will take notes during these times and will share them with you. Your child will be asked to do activities alone or with a group, and I will report on the success of these activities. Finally, I will keep track of skills your child has mastered on a progressive list of skills.

One goal of my assessment of your child is to provide rich information about his or her progress. Your child's portfolio will open up a continuing dialogue between parent, student, and teacher concerning what your child needs to succeed. Another goal is to help your child become an independent, self-directed learner. Putting together a portfolio encourages your child to take responsibility for his or her learning, which is something effective learners do throughout their whole lives.

Sincerely,

Book Orders

Dear Parents:

The book order forms are here. Attached you will find an order form for some great books you may wish to purchase for your child. These forms will be sent home monthly. It is always optional to place a book order.

Building up your child's library is one of the best ways to contribute to your child's education. Other ways you can stock your child's personal library are by frequently visiting the library; mentioning to grandmas, aunts, and uncles that books make great gifts; and swapping books with friends. Does your child have a bookshelf? If not, it's time to put one together to communicate the importance of reading to your child.

Remembering these tips will help me greatly in processing your child's book order.

- Make a check payable to the book club on the order form. Please do not write the check out to me or the school, and please do not send cash.
- Put your child's name in the appropriate place on the order form.
- Put the check and order form in an envelope labeled with your child's name and room number.
- Return the order form to me by _____.

Some items you may want to take a special look at in this month's book order are:

When the books come in, take the time to read them enthusiastically with your child. Popular children's author Mem Fox believes that when we read books to children, we share a little bit of life together. Happy reading and happy sharing!

Sincerely,

Centers

Dear Parents:

Centers time is a joyous time in our classroom. It is a time of great activity and learning. During centers time, the students are offered a wide variety of activities from which to choose. The benefits of centers are:

Planning. Each student plans beforehand which centers will be visited. This helps a child's organizational skills and teaches a child to set and evaluate goals.

Choice. Children are encouraged to visit a variety of centers, but in the end the choice of which center to visit is theirs. Students who learn how to make choices in the early years feel more in control of their learning and therefore will become more self-directed. Children are drawn to the center they need, even if it is "Day 148 at the block table." It is the quality of the activity that is important.

Risk taking. During centers time, children are allowed to make mistakes and learn from them on their own. Centers time allows them time to test their budding abilities without fear.

Discovery! The hands-on nature of centers lends itself to innumerable discoveries. Great math and science discoveries can be made in just one day at the water table, for example.

Language. A room with centers is abuzz with conversation. Children try out new vocabulary in a safe environment of play.

Social skills. Students learn to share, take turns, solve problems, negotiate, give and accept compliments, and respect other children, among other social skills learned during centers time. Our increasingly interdependent world makes these skills paramount for children to learn.

I communicate to the children that they must be working on something during centers time. This encourages good work habits for future years. If your child at this age can take a block of time and plan, make valuable choices, and keep occupied during that time while using social skills, he or she is truly preparing for later school years.

Centers can be a noisy time. This does not mean learning is not taking place. I have heard it said that silence should be justified in a primary classroom, not noise. Productive noise will fill our classroom as the students reach toward greater learning through centers.

Sincerely,

Letter 3.5

Classroom Procedures

Dear Parents:

You may or may not have heard your child mention "procedures" from school. We talk about them every day, and they are part of what helps our classroom run so smoothly. Procedures are the behaviors and skills I expect from your child throughout the day. Different from rules, procedures describe how to do a given action such as how to get help from the teacher and what to do when finished with a task. We spent a lot of time the first few weeks of school mapping out how to talk appropriately in class, how to move around the room, and how to get bathroom and drink needs met along with other routine activities. The key is to let the students know exactly how to negotiate any task that might come up.

Students feel more secure when they know what is expected of them. In addition, I am very consistent with procedures, which also leads to further security. We have discussed the "whys" of each procedure, and so they make sense to the students. It helps me to be more objective with them: If there is a problem, I refer the student back to our clearly defined classroom procedures. The use of procedures cuts down on discipline issues and allows my students more time to learn.

You can help by reinforcing the concept of procedures at home. Jane Nelson, in her 1996 book *Positive Discipline,* refers to this as "taking time for training." Discipline problems in the classroom and at home can occur when adults assume children know all the steps to accomplishing a task. Following are some activities that might lend themselves to defining procedures or taking time for training at home:

Cleaning one's room	Making a sandwich
Doing the dishes	Setting the table
Laying out clothes	Putting away toys
Playing with the dog	Inviting friends over

Developing procedures takes time, but the time and arguments saved by having clear expectations is well worth the initial investment. Using procedures helps eliminate power struggles, because the focus is on behavior and not on the child. In other words, procedures keep things from getting personal. With teacher and parental support, your child will reap many benefits by being exposed to procedures and high expectations.

Sincerely,

Letter 3.6

Cooperative Learning

Dear Parents:

There is not just one teacher in this class. There are many, as every student in the class has something to share and the ability to help others learn. For this reason, we often break into cooperative learning groups. I view cooperative learning as more than just throwing kids together in a group and expecting them to learn. Our groups are formed around these ideas:

Group interdependence. For a group to be effective, each member must feel that he or she has a role in the group, and that as a group, the children will "sink or swim" together. The minute one member feels his or her efforts are not needed, that child will hold back those efforts. Therefore, I often assign group roles, and monitor the groups to be sure each child is engaged.

Lots of verbal exchange. About 15 times more discussion occurs in cooperative learning groups than in a whole class grouping. The amount of time a child spends explaining something is directly related to the amount that child learns.

Individual accountability. Tasks are structured so that the group can only be successful if every member contributes. Every member of the group is responsible for something, and students are later assessed as individuals. This is called group-to-individual transfer and is very important when cooperative learning is used.

Processing. The students will always take time at the end of a cooperative lesson to talk about what went well and what did not. Discussing the content learned doubles retention of that concept.

Developing social skills. Students in cooperative groups learn social skills such as listening, encouraging, negotiating, and respecting individual differences among many others. I take time to teach these skills directly since they rarely come naturally.

Cooperative activities involve higher-level reasoning and allow students to think in ways they might not be ready to on their own. Cooperative learning has been studied for over 90 years, and most studies show achievement to be higher in cooperative settings than in competitive or individual settings. Perhaps a better argument for cooperative learning, however, is the social gains children make in groups. In a 1983 study by the Center for Public Resources, *Basic Skills in the U.S. Work Force,* 90% of firings of workers were due to interpersonal problems, poor job attitudes, and inappropriate behavior. Cooperative learning helps students to learn necessary social skills that will stay with them for a lifetime.

Sincerely,

How Children Are Grouped

Dear Parents:

During the day, your child has an opportunity to work with a whole class, individually, and in small groups. These groups might take the form of the following:

Skill groups. I will work with small groups of children who all need instruction on the same skill, such as handwriting a certain letter or working on a math concept.

Interest groups. At times, children will form a work group based on a common interest. A group interested in football, for example, may do a language activity relating to that sport.

The well-known ability groups are used sparingly in my classroom. Here are some of the reasons why:

1. Ability grouping does not promote achievement and actually depresses learning for all but those in top groups.
2. Students in top-ability groups are shown to achieve about the same whether ability grouped or not.
3. Ability groups are often permanent. In one study, children were grouped eight days after the start of kindergarten. By the second grade, none of the children had moved from his or her grouping.
4. Ability grouping leads to labeling children and results in decreased self-esteem.
5. Often, groupings are made on the basis of a fixed idea of ability, ignoring the fact that all children have different strengths and weaknesses. In addition, children mature at different rates and sudden bursts of maturity occur often.

This is not to say I won't take a group of children with similar ability levels aside for instruction. What I will do is keep these groupings flexible, never label the groups, and keep a close eye on all my students' progress for grouping purposes. In addition, I will maintain high but reachable expectations for all students. My lessons are structured to reach a variety of ability levels, which reduces the need for ability grouping. Last, offering a rich curriculum with lots of hands-on learning goes a long way toward meeting your child's needs as an individual.

Sincerely,

Inclusion of Students With Special Needs

Dear Parents:

Every student is reachable and teachable. This is a belief held at our school, and that is why children with special needs are members in our classrooms. This practice, called inclusion, involves giving students with special needs the opportunity to belong in regular classrooms as much as possible. Students with special needs such as physical and mental disabilities grow tremendously when placed in a classroom with nondisabled children. However, nondisabled children also reap these great rewards:

New friendships. Nondisabled children experience friendships that have a different character than they are used to. When a friend with special needs is successful, the nondisabled friend feels a part of that success.

Increased self-esteem. Working with a child with special needs puts some children in a leadership role they might not otherwise find themselves in.

Advanced social skills. Increased understanding and an awareness of the needs of others results when disabled students are in the classroom. Patience is another common side effect.

Greater comfort level. Exposure to children with special needs breaks down the fear some children have of people with physical or mental disabilities. Parents have noted their comfort level also increased as a result of inclusion.

Development of personal principles. Children exposed to the disabled today will grow to be their advocates tomorrow.

Some parents are concerned about the effect special needs children will have on their own child's academic growth. Thankfully, studies have failed to show any slowdown in the learning of nondisabled children in inclusive classrooms. To ensure my students experience the same success, I will take time to teach social skills to all the children. I will model acceptance of all children, with and without disabilities. Finally, I will monitor the amount of time nondisabled children assume helping roles in the classroom. The growth of all my students is my first priority, and it is my commitment to make inclusion a beneficial practice in my classroom for all students.

Sincerely,

Multiage Groupings

Dear Parents:

Our multiage classroom is not an experiment or a fad. It is based on 25 years of research and has its roots deep in history. School groupings were multiage, as in the one-room schoolhouse, until the turn of the century when schoolchildren began to go to school in large numbers. Placing children in grades was part of the efficiency practices of the industrial revolution. An assembly line model of education is clearly inappropriate for your child today.

Multiage classes usually consist of groups of children who have an age span of at least a year. They are designed to resemble family and neighborhood groupings, where people of all ages play and learn together. Multiage classes are based on the premise that all children have different interests and skill levels, and these differences may not have to do with age. In other words, each child in a multiage class is viewed as an individual and progresses along a continuum of learning at his or her own pace.

Some of the features of multiage classes are:

Rich curriculum. Multiage classes relax the rigid curriculum used in single-age classes, which are usually designed for the "average" student. The "average" curriculum bores some children and frustrates others. Multiage classes focus on the child, not the curriculum. Single-age classes assume children will learn the same things, in the same way, at the same pace. In multiage classes, lessons are designed to meet a variety of skill levels, catching students at their individual level.

The expert-novice relationship. Children learn from interacting with each other. Older children in a grouping learn leadership skills. They strengthen their skills and knowledge already acquired by leading and instructing younger children. Younger children learn from older role models, and their language levels rise to meet the older children's level. Younger children in multiage classrooms engage in more interactive, as opposed to side-by-side, play.

Social skills flourish. The diversity of ages allows children to be helpful, patient, and tolerant. By interacting with younger peers, older children have increased motivation and self-confidence. Older children teach younger children classroom rules, and that seems to help older children internalize and follow those rules.

Recipe for success. Multiage classes minimize the possibility of children "failing" a grade. Academic failure is less likely to occur, because students progress at their own pace. A cooperative environment eliminates behavior problems that come with competition. In multiage classrooms, being different is the norm, and your child's differences will be honored and capitalized on in our classroom.

Sincerely,

On Curriculum

Parents are more able to help with schoolwork when they understand your curriculum and its philosophy. Parents want to know how you go about teaching their children, and these letters answer their many questions. Each letter in this section gives parents concrete ways to support their child's education at home.

Rationale for Sending Home These Letters

A Balanced Reading Program Letter. Parents have heard much through the media and other sources about whole language versus phonics-based approaches to teaching reading. Use this letter to communicate to parents that you use what works with children: an approach that uses both phonics instruction and a whole language philosophy designed to reach all children.

Comprehension Letter. Sometimes people forget the true purpose of reading: comprehension. This letter invites parents to help children "dig a little deeper" when reading by using higher-order thinking skills and comprehension strategies.

Functional Writing Experiences Letter. Since writing develops best when used in real-life situations, this letter gives parents ideas for authentic writing experiences at home.

Spelling, K–1 Letter. Parents have widely differing opinions about invented spelling. The benefits of invented spelling and the progression to standard spelling are described in this letter.

Spelling, 2–3 Letter. Many parents were taught spelling with the weekly spelling test. This letter shifts the emphasis from "passing Friday's test" to using strategies to spell words correctly in real writing.

What Is Math? Letter. It's not the new math, or the old math, but math that works that is described in this letter. The letter also explains the uses of manipulatives and the role of basic math facts in an effective math program.

What Is Reading? K–1 Letter. Reading is not merely a matter of putting sounds together. This letter explains how the three cuing systems—grapho-phonic, semantic, and syntactic—work together to make meaning. It also lists reading readiness concepts.

What Is Reading? 2–3 Letter. This letter also describes the three cuing systems and then goes on to speak about the kinds of books children at this age benefit from reading.

A Balanced Reading Program

Dear Parents:

Balance is a positive term (balanced diet, balanced lifestyle), and it is one I use to describe my reading program. There is much talk lately about a whole language approach versus a phonics-based approach to teaching reading. I balance the two approaches, thereby using whatever works to help young children learn to read.

Whole language, although difficult to define, means instruction that emphasizes reading for meaning, the use of children's literature as opposed to textbooks, early writing, projects arising from students' interests, and the teaching of skills in the context of real reading. Children who do well in whole language environments often have global reading styles. They can recall words from stories, and writing helps them learn to read.

Phonics-based instruction emphasizes letter-sound relationships and patterns. This approach involves textbooks, teacher-directed lessons, workbooks, and lots of drill and practice. Students who do well with a phonics-based approach have auditory and analytic reading styles. Auditory children can hear and remember sounds. The logic of phonics appeals to this type of analytic learner.

Offering a balanced program is the only way to reach each student. Global thinkers are easily bored with phonics and don't see the connections. Analytical thinkers see whole language as disorganized. The bottom line is, all children need to be exposed to great literature and all children can benefit from phonics instruction. Phonics is a tool for making meaning, and whole language is a framework for learning how to read.

Since an estimated 20% of students will have difficulty with phonological awareness (knowing letter sounds and how to blend them), phonics activities are important. Signs of poor phonological awareness include difficulty with rhyming tasks, inability to divide words into syllables, or reading slowly or inaccurately. Activities to help boost this awareness are:

- Repeating nursery rhymes
- Games:
  "What sounds do you hear in the word _____?"
  "Is there a letter ___ in the word _____?"
  "What is the first sound in _____?"
- Helping your child to blend words:
  "What sounds do /c/ /a/ /t/ make?"
- Counting syllables by placing a hand under the chin and counting the movements in a word

The most important goal is to encourage your child to want to read. A balanced approach to reading instruction offers your child the best chance at meeting this goal.

Sincerely,

Comprehension

Dear Parents:

It is wonderful to watch children read fluently. It is important to remember this is but one piece of the pie. The real goal of reading is to understand, or comprehend, the words on the page. Comprehension is a skill that needs cultivation, like playing the piano or learning to play baseball. There are a lots of "ins and outs" in learning to get the most out of reading, but thankfully they're not difficult to encourage.

Retelling. Ask your child from time to time to retell a story as if telling it to a friend who has never heard the story before. This helps children with knowledge of story structure.

Going beyond the obvious. There are several levels of comprehension. They are:

- Literal: Asking questions such as "What color was the dog?" The answers to literal questions can be found right in the text.
- Interpretive: "Why did Mrs. Peterson put the dog outside?" is an interpretive question. The answers to these questions are not directly stated but would be agreed upon by most readers.
- Critical: A critical question could be "Why did the author make Jaime leave the party early?" There may be a variety of answers.
- Evaluative: These are questions that tap at what did and did not appeal to the reader. "What words did you like that described the character?" is an evaluative question.

Helping your child to question. Help your child design "Big 3" questions to go with a story:

"What do you think . . . ?"
"Why do you think . . . ?"
"How do you feel . . . ?"

By encouraging your child to dig a little deeper, we are helping to root story structure more firmly in your child's mind. Teaching your child to think on a higher level about literature is a skill that will help him or her to get more out of reading and will contribute to lifelong reading.

Sincerely,

Functional Writing Experiences

Dear Parents:

Children enjoy writing when there is a purpose for doing so. When children need and want to communicate with printed words, their skills develop as a result. Opportunities for real writing can be found all around your home. Following are some activities you might want to encourage at home:

Letters to relatives	Shopping lists
Telephone messages	Notes to friends
Recipes	Invitations
Holiday cards	Notes to the teacher
Travel diary	Daily journal
Menus	Captions for photo album

Your child will be doubly rewarded when writing for free samples, travel brochures, or any other types of information. Not only will writing skills develop through this activity, but your child will experience the power of getting a response to his or her communications.

Write notes to your child and put them in various places (in lunch boxes, on the refrigerator, under pillows, and in back pockets). Encourage your child to write back to you. This is a fun way to increase your child's writing fluency and for you to be a writing model for your child.

It is important for your child to know that writing does not occur only in the classroom and that writing has a purpose and can be fun.

Sincerely,

Letter 4.4

Spelling, K–1

Dear Parents:

"I luv u, mom!" A child writing this is in one of the early stages of spelling. Spelling follows a developmental progression, which is described below:

1. Random letters: Students use letters to communicate, but they don't correspond with sounds. (YHGTDRSXF = "I went to the store.")
2. Consonants: Students use one letter, usually the first one in a word. (M D M P = "My dad makes pancakes.")
3. Initial and final consonants: Students use the first and last sounds in words. (I WT SM MR CS = "I want some more crayons.")
4. Vowel/consonant combinations: Consonant and vowel sounds are used in the middle of words. (MI BES FRD IS JONE = "My best friend is Johnny.")
5. Words: All the sounds are represented. (I WAS RUNING WEN I FEL = "I was running when I fell.")
6. Standard spelling: Children have a large bank of sight words and knowledge of spelling patterns. (I CAN SPELL! = "I can spell!")

In the beginning stages, children use developmental or "invented" spelling. This is to be encouraged, rather than viewed as mistaken spelling. At this stage in literacy, invented spelling is a technique for children to learn more about letter sounds and the written word. Greater writing gains are made by children who are allowed to play with language this way. As a process of phonics, it helps children develop phonemic awareness, which will actually make them better spellers in the long run.

Invented spelling also tells a lot about a child's particular stage of spelling development. If a child is using random letters, some instruction on letter sounds is necessary. If the letter *p* is being used to write the word *bubbles,* some activities on the difference between *p* and *b* are in order. If a child is only using initial consonants, directing that child to listen for ending sounds would be helpful.

Using invented spelling does not mean standard spelling is not important. It definitely is. Using the stages of spelling listed above, we can follow your child's progression as he or she gradually lets go of invented spelling and starts to use standard spelling. This progression cannot be rushed but can be guided by talking about words, letting your child play with them, and immersing your child in literacy.

Sincerely,

Spelling, 2–3

Dear Parents:

An estimated 15% to 20% of Americans are poor spellers. With that in mind, your child's development in spelling right now is very important. Spelling is not an end but a means for making writing easier, more fluent, and more expressive. Therefore, the goal of my spelling program is for students to be able to use correct spelling in their daily writing.

Teaching spelling is more complex than giving a Friday spelling test on words learned during a week. It is actually a conceptual process, as opposed to one of memorization. Friday spelling tests don't guarantee spelling words are learned, but effective spelling instruction does. Following are some components of my program:

High-frequency words. One hundred words make up half of all the words we use in writing. One thousand words make up 90% of all written words we use. Therefore, we focus on high-frequency words. If children are misspelling basic words, it makes no sense to teach them words they rarely use.

Word families. Right, might, fight, and light are easier to learn once you know the pattern.

Individual words. Students are motivated by being able to choose some special words to learn. Please honor your child's choices.

Spelling skills. Your child will receive instruction on prefixes, suffixes, syllables, alphabetical order, compound words, and base words. Knowledge of these skills makes spelling easier.

Spelling aids. Spelling correctly involves learning to use a dictionary and thesaurus, learning to proofread, and learning different methods (visual, tactile) for learning to spell new words.

Writing, writing, writing. And reading, reading, reading, too! Children learn to spell by seeing words, talking about them, writing words, and playing with them. Frequent reading and writing are directly related to spelling ability.

Students are most interested in spelling words they need to communicate correctly. Therefore, opportunities for real writing offer reinforcement in spelling. Letters to grandma or a favorite cousin, shopping or gift lists, phone messages, a diary, invitations, and thank you letters are examples of real writing that will develop spelling.

I welcome your participation and questions about our spelling program. Please feel free to contact me.

Sincerely,

What Is Math?

Dear Parents:

"I see, and I forget. I hear, and I remember. I do, and I understand." This Chinese proverb sums up what is happening in math today. The main goal in our classroom is to develop true understanding of math concepts as they relate to the real world. Kids succeed when they see math as an aspect of their daily lives. Many of us learned the concept of division with remainders by sharing four cookies with three friends. Children in the primary years have formed math concepts from such experiences and need help in putting a label on these experiences ("I used division—four divided by three is one, with a remainder of one").

One way to develop understanding is through manipulatives. Manipulatives are items that can be held by hand, or manipulated, to help a child solve a problem. One student might use buttons to add numbers together, another might make a pattern with colored shapes, still another might divide a cookie into fractions. Manipulatives make abstract concepts tangible and actually allow children to solve problems they might not be otherwise ready to solve. Classrooms that rely on paper-and-pencil activities actually delay growth in math learning. Through manipulatives, kids can test their math reasoning, which develops their ability and confidence. In addition, hands-on learning leads to greater retention of math concepts.

The math concepts children learn today extend far beyond addition, subtraction, multiplication, and division. These four areas, referred to as computation, make up part of the total math curriculum, of which the main focus is problem solving. Other activities your child will be involved in include estimation (which builds up common sense about numbers), data collection and statistics (which will help children learn to process the flood of information they will face daily), geometry, measuring, and patterning (which is a cornerstone of mathematics).

Basic math facts are not ignored, however. Often, children who have difficulty in math are lagging because of the amount of time it takes them to do the computation in a problem, although they solve the problem correctly. Therefore, it is important to learn basic math facts automatically. But computation should not be seen as an end but rather as a tool in the development of problem-solving ability.

The National Council of Teachers of Mathematics recommends explorations that sustain children's curiosity and enjoyment of mathematics. This group also strongly advocates building up children's confidence in math. Math anxiety is far too common and can be alleviated by relating math lessons to students' experiences. We will also be talking and writing about math in our classroom, which will help your child to learn the language of mathematics. The end result will be students who are comfortable, active problem solvers with a real feel for numbers and what they mean.

Sincerely,

What Is Reading? K–1

Dear Parents:

The world of books is opening up for your child. In the next year, your child will show gains in literacy that will be exciting to watch. A necessary starting point on this journey is to clearly define reading. Reading is basically using printed symbols in a search for meaning. The goal is to understand the printed word, not merely pronounce words properly. To accomplish this, readers use three cuing systems:

The grapho-phonic system. This is the system most people are familiar with. It involves knowing letter sounds and how to blend them to read words and sentences. Often, the grapho-phonic system is referred to as phonics. It is but one way to read unfamiliar words.

The semantic system. "She _____ the door and went inside." We know the word is "opened," because it makes sense in the sentence. The semantic system uses the context of the known words to help figure out the unfamiliar ones.

The syntactic system. This system relies on what sounds right grammatically. In the sentence "The boy _____ the man." We know the word would be "helps" as opposed to "help," because of the way the sentence sounds.

As your child begins to read, all three of these cuing systems will be used to help "crack the code" of written language. But knowing the code is not enough. Children have to want to use the code to become lifelong readers. My goal is to help your child see reading as rewarding. We are living in an ever-increasing "aliterate" society, meaning people can read but don't choose to. We need to communicate to your child that life is richer with the printed word.

There are a few prerequisite concepts for reading. Your child needs to know the following:

- There is a difference between words and pictures.
- Words have meaning.
- Words on a page progress from left to right.
- Words are made up by letters and are separated by spaces.
- Letters come in upper-case and lower-case form.

Assuming these concepts are in place, your child is ready to learn more about reading. However, it is more important for a child to learn to read well than to be the first reader on the block. Early readers do level off, as other students catch up with them eventually. Therefore, it's best to have reasonable expectations, follow your child's lead, and gently but consistently support literacy development by reading to him or her and providing language-rich experiences.

Sincerely,

What Is Reading? 2–3

Dear Parents:

The world of books is in your child's hands. This is an exciting time. In the next year, your child will make great leaps in reading fluency and comprehension. A necessary starting point on this journey is to clearly define reading. Reading is basically using printed symbols in a search for meaning. The goal is to understand the printed word, not merely pronounce words properly. To accomplish this, readers use three cuing systems to help make meaning from text:

The grapho-phonic system. This is the system most people are familiar with. It involves knowing letter sounds and how to blend them to read words and sentences. Often, the grapho-phonic system is referred to as phonics. It is but one way to read unfamiliar words.

The semantic system. "She _____ the door and went inside." We know the word is "opened," because it makes sense in the sentence. The semantic system uses the context of the known words to help figure out the unfamiliar ones.

The syntactic system. This system relies on what sounds right grammatically. In the sentence "The boy _____ the man," we know the word would be "helps" as opposed to "help," because of the way the sentence sounds.

As your child begins to read, all three of these cuing systems will be used to help "crack the code" of written language. But knowing the code is not enough. Children have to want to use the code to become lifelong readers. My goal is to help your child see reading as rewarding. We are living in an ever-increasing "aliterate" society, meaning people can read but don't choose to. Eighty percent of the books in this country are read by 10% of the population. We need to communicate to your child that life is richer with the printed word. We can do this by exposing your child to

- Literature that fires them up about language and all its delights
- Books that celebrate diversity and respect differences
- Books that demonstrate the value of literacy
- A variety of books: fiction, nonfiction, biography, poetry, and more

Children at your child's age benefit from being taught to be active readers—to always question, predict, reread, relate to their own experience, and summarize in the process of reading. It's an exciting ride, one I am glad to be going on with your child.

Sincerely,

For Building
Home-School Partnerships

Parents want to know specifically what they can do at home to support their children's education. Therefore, parents will greatly appreciate the letters in this section. The suggestions contained in the letters are easy to implement, and they guide parents to work on higher-level skills and concepts.

Rationale for
Sending Home These Letters

Appreciating Children's Art Letter. Specific comments about a child's artwork from adults can either spur a child on to create more or squelch creativity, depending on the comment. This letter advises what to say and what not to say when looking at a child's masterpiece.

How to Help With Math Letter. Math opportunities are abundant around the home. By showing how to use household numbers to practice math, you will be helping your students apply the math skills and concepts they learn at school.

How to Help With Reading Letter. This letter encourages parents to help their children with reading through joyful pursuits. Reading is presented as being intertwined with speaking, listening, and writing.

How to Help With Writing Letter. Parents are directed to see writing as both an art and a craft in this letter. Parents are asked to resign as "grammar editor," and instead focus on the meaning in their children's writing.

Making the Most Out of a Trip to the Library Letter. This letter gives structure to trips to the library. It also gives suggestions for choosing appropriate books for a child. Sources for lists of children's books are included.

Science at Home Letter. Home is a great place for science. Included in this letter are science experiments children can easily perform at home. It directs parents to capitalize on their children's curiosity.

Summer Activities Letter. Parents are most grateful for ideas they can use with their children over summer break. This list emphasizes fun activities that are also educational.

Television Letter. "TV kids" don't do as well in school as those who watch television moderately. This letter tells how to use TV wisely in the home.

Appreciating Children's Art

Dear Parents:

"Do you like my picture?" These five words can paralyze a parent looking at a picture that could be a house or a map of Australia, depending on how you hold it. But it is important to learn how to look at children's artwork so that you can give truly helpful feedback. The main goal in responding to children's artwork is to guide the child to see value in his or her work and to inspire the child to create again. It's easier to start with what not to say when faced with a piece of art:

"I love it!" This puts the focus on you as a judge of the child's work. Artists follow their hearts. Say to your child, "What do you think of your work? You are the artist."

"What is it?" It's true—many times an adult can't tell what a child has created. "Tell me about this part" will give you the information you need.

"Don't you think your picture needs . . . ?" Young children don't need to approximate reality. Unless teaching an art lesson, comments such as these dampen creativity.

"It's nice!" Fluffy, not meaningful, insincere, and the child can sense this. On the flip side, it's best not to go on and on about artwork that may have taken the child less than 30 seconds to create. Your credibility will be in question.

Thankfully, there are a few key things to look for in your child's work:

- Comment on what the artwork is made of (watercolor, sand and glue, clay).
- Find parts that interest you, such as the bold streak of yellow through the center or the torn pieces of paper glued on the side.
- Ask your child where the idea for the artwork came from.
- Ask your child what the piece is about, or if it tells a story.
- Ask any other open-ended, nonjudgmental questions about the artwork.
- Comment on the effort that went into the artwork.

Kids want our approval. The challenge is teach your child to create for himself or herself. Using the above questions and comments leads your child to evaluate his or her own art, which is what great artists do.

Sincerely,

How to Help With Math

Dear Parents:

By the fourth grade, most children have formed attitudes toward math that will last throughout their lives. If a child's attitude is a positive one, math instruction will be stimulating and rewarding. A negative attitude spells frustrating years of math classes and a diminished number of career options. Therefore, the early years are crucial in developing positive attitudes toward math.

The home is an ideal place to practice math concepts, because numbers are all around. Just one session in the kitchen can teach addition and subtraction of fractions, estimating, measurement, multiplication (four rows of three cookies on a tray equals 12 cookies) to name just a few. When your child helps you measure a window for curtains, estimates how many glasses can go in the dishwasher, or makes a graph of phone calls received in a day, he or she is learning math concepts that will stick.

Children as young as three and four can subtract, although this concept isn't introduced until much later, and even at a later age some children struggle with the concept. A four-year-old has experienced having a handful of cookies and giving some away, or having a box of crayons and loaning some to friends. They have had the experience of subtraction but have not experienced the language of subtraction ("You had three cookies and gave two away. Three minus two is one"). This is where you can help. Whenever you see your child manipulating numbers, identify what the child has done. This is called *naming,* and this creates a link between what the child knows intuitively and what that child knows consciously.

In the early years, children are developing a number sense. This is more than just being able to count, which doesn't guarantee a knowledge of what numbers mean. Number sense is developed when children lay out their own clothes (one shirt, two socks), set the table (four family members = four forks, eight corn holders), consult the calendar (eight more days until winter), or plant seeds (eight seeds in four rows equals 32 plants). Children at this age are also learning about patterns, which is really what math is all about. While you are in the grocery store, ask your child to look for patterns (tile patterns on the floor, patterns on cereal boxes, patterns in the colors of fruits or vegetables, patterns of lit-up check-out aisles).

Another skill that lends itself to home learning is estimation, which again builds up number sense. Ask your child, "How many bowls will that box of cereal fill?" If your child says 50, you know more estimation activities are in order. Children improve their estimation ability quickly with practice, and this can be a joy to watch. Estimation helps children in later years to decide if their answers to problems are reasonable. Home math learning should most of all be fun. It allows kids to see math as part of their daily lives, which will lead to a lifelong positive attitude about mathematics.

Sincerely,

How to Help With Reading

Dear Parents:

I am often asked by parents how they can help their child with reading. The very first place to start is with yourself, by being a literacy role model for your child. If you let your child catch you reading, your child will see reading as valuable. Your child will see that reading is pleasurable as well as useful. Another way to help is to be a vocabulary role model. Use and introduce your child to new words often. Make a game out of saying the same thing with different words. You'll know you've made progress when you hear your child using new vocabulary in play situations.

It is very important to read to your child daily. Just as important as reading to your child is to have your child read or tell you a story. Children love to have their developing skills appreciated by an admired adult. The more pleasurable the reading experiences your child has, the greater his or her motivation to read will be. Your role in reading with your child is simple: Be patient and playful. This approach nurtures reading development.

Here are a few literacy activities your child can do at home:

- Write or dictate stories
- Keep a diary
- Act out parts of a story
- Make up stories using familiar characters
- Make a shopping list
- Write letters or postcards to relatives
- Help with the cooking
- Play rhyming or letter sound games
- Read more than just books—T-shirts, cereal boxes, street signs, and so on
- Read a morning message written by mom or dad
- Visit the local public library often

Engage your child in any activity where there is a need to read to get information. When students understand the reasons for reading, they are more likely to become lifelong readers.

By providing your child with a wide range of reading materials, you are communicating the importance of reading. Through the library or bookstores, fill up your child's personal library with books that have a span of three to four grade levels. In addition, have books everywhere—in the kitchen and the bathroom, or wherever else your child might have a moment to pick up a book.

Another factor influencing reading achievement is television. Research shows that after about 11 hours of weekly TV watching, achievement scores drop. The quality of what your child is watching is also a factor. Two other factors associated with high reading ability are more time spent doing chores and more time eating as a family at the dinner table. These are areas to look at when trying to help your child succeed.

Sincerely,

How to Help With Writing

Dear Parents:

Writing is an art, one that we will be refining each day in class. It is also a craft, which we will be spending much time learning. You can help your child in the following ways:

As an art. As a painter needs a studio, palettes, and brushes, provide your child with an area for writing and have plenty of materials ready:

Pencils and pens	A desk lamp (100-watt bulb)
Pads of paper	Envelopes
A dictionary	A thesaurus
Stamps	A diary

Provide your child with as many rich experiences and lively conversations as possible to build up your child's vocabulary and a store of topics to write about.

As a craft. The goal of writing is to communicate. Therefore, show your child how you communicate through writing. Share letters you receive from friends and relatives. Talk out loud while you are writing and explain your word choices. Focus on the meaning of your child's writing by responding in the following ways:

Mirroring: "I enjoyed the part about the drawbridge."
Questioning: "What would have happened if the bridge wasn't lifted?"
Connecting: "Remember that book about castles we read?"

Don't take on the job of editor of your child's writing (or resign from it if you already have). Children are helped more when parents focus on the content of what their child has written as opposed to the grammar. Writing development is a slow process in the early years; the skills are not all learned at once. And, as in learning to play the piano, many sour notes need to be plunked out before a beautiful sonata can be played. In addition, for every error you find on your child's page, you will probably be able to find 10 things your child did well. You will nurture your child's writing by encouraging his or her efforts.

Children learn to write by writing, but also by reading. The more exposure your child has to print, the more naturally writing ability will develop.

Sincerely,

Making the Most Out of a Trip to the Library

Dear Parents:

We all know taking a child to the library can be a great experience. The challenge is to make the most of the time spent there. The first step is to get to know the children's librarian. The children's librarian is an unlimited source of information. If your child needs a book on the three-toed sloth, the librarian will find it in an instant.

Here are some guidelines for helping your child choose books he or she will enjoy and be successful with:

Know your child's interests. Teach your child to find books on favorite topics by using the card catalog. Capitalize on your child's interests, as motivation leads to more reading. In fact, be an advocate for your child's interests by valuing them and supporting them, even if one of them is the three-toed sloth. This will continue a positive cycle of self-esteem associated with reading.

Look at the characters. Children should read about other kids who can solve problems. It is valuable for children to find their counterparts as well as role models in books.

Follow your child's lead. Allow your child to pick books that perhaps don't fit his or her gender stereotype. Also, it is not necessary to only pick books at your child's grade level. Assigning books a grade level is for instructional purposes only.

Consider developmental level. The under-six set likes predictable pattern books with bold illustrations. Six- to nine-year-old children seek stories with morals.

Teach your child to scan. Show your child how to read the book jacket and how to skim through a few pages to determine a book's suitability.

When children are reading on their own, a good rule of thumb is the 75-90 rule. For a book to be readable, it helps if the child comprehends 75% of the information on the page and can read correctly 90% of the words (less than one error for every 10 words). Two organizations that offer current lists of good books for children are:

Children's Book Council   American Library Association
67 Irving Place   50 East Huron Street
New York, NY 10003   Chicago, IL 60611

Remember to send a self-addressed, stamped envelope with your request. A trip to the library can be a productive experience. Happy Reading!

Sincerely,

Letter 5.6

Science at Home

Dear Parents:

Plato said, "All philosophy begins in wonder." Developing a sense of wonder in your child is a main goal of our science program this year. Children, being curious, are natural scientists. Our job is to encourage your child's curiosity and build on it through providing time and space for scientific explorations.

The beauty of science is that it can be found everywhere. In fact, the best place to start is with the child's world. Children want to know how things work and why. By focusing on the questions that occur to them, children see science as an understandable part of life. Real-life science surrounds us—from observing the number of birds that visit a feeder to watching what happens when a rock hits a puddle. Your child's environment is rich with possibilities for discovery, and you can help by:

1. Following your child's lead. Resist answering questions if there is some way the child could answer them through exploration. If it is a question your child could find the answer to, provide encouragement and whatever materials may be necessary.
2. Asking open-ended questions that can lead in many directions. "What if . . . ?" questions stimulate scientific pursuits.
3. Building up a tolerance for slimy, furry, scaly, thorny things. Any aversion you may have could be passed on to your child and might discourage some scientific discovery.
4. Taking a nonsexist approach to science. Communicate its importance for both girls and boys.
5. Building up your child's personal library to include books on science.

Your child can practice the process skills of observing, communicating, classifying, predicting, inferring, and measuring by taking part in the following home experiments:

- Leaving out a piece of bread
- Timing an ice cube as it melts
- Measuring bubbles
- Predicting dinner based on smell
- Staring at the night sky
- Walking in the park using the senses
- Recording and charting the weather
- Going on a rock and fossil hunt
- Watering a plant with juice
- Seeing which items will sink and float
- Measuring shadow length
- Feeling the temperature of objects
- Anything else your child wants to explore

Sincerely,

Letter 5.7

Summer Activities

Dear Parents:

Where has the year gone? I have truly enjoyed working with all your children, and I will miss them over our summer break. I have some suggestions for activities your child will enjoy this summer that will also keep his or her skills sharp. Few of the activities involve formal schoolwork. However, all of the activities do promote learning:

Cooking. Through cooking, children learn math, science, social studies, and language skills while satisfying their tummies at the same time. Cooking is probably the richest daily educational experience your child can have. Time spent in the kitchen is well worth the effort.

Gardening. Summertime is prime time for getting reacquainted with the great outdoors. Your child can predict what will grow, do all sorts of math with seeds, measure and chart plant growth, read about plants, and write to relatives about the garden. Gardening teaches children in a fast-food world that not everything can be ready in five minutes.

Music. Your child can take up a musical instrument, or make musical instruments with materials found around the home (a facial tissue box and rubber band make a guitar, a paper towel roll makes a horn). Give a child a tape recorder, microphone, and a blank tape and you won't see that child for hours. (But you will probably hear the results—over and over again.)

Library. Check out the local library's summer reading program. Make visiting the library a weekly affair. It's cool inside, with lots of cool books.

Water play. Toss water balloons, play musical buckets (using buckets of water instead of chairs), play kiddie pool tug-of-war, pretend to paint on the sidewalk or fence with paintbrushes and a bucket of water, or just play with a garden hose. Water is a fascinating springboard for science explorations.

Writing. Your child can keep a summer diary. Writing to friends and relatives can be fun, especially when getting letters in return.

Managing money. If your child doesn't already have one, help him or her set up a system for tracking money received from an allowance, gifts, or the tooth fairy. There's nothing quite like cold, hard cash to teach math skills. Students learn four quarters equal a dollar long before they understand fractions.

Language and math games. When the time is right (in the car, while waiting in line), challenge your child to a game or brain teaser. The summertime rule is, however, make it fun.

Sincerely,

Television

Dear Parents:

The average high school graduate will have spent 11,000 hours in the classroom and 15,000 hours in front of the television. The average child is said to watch five to six hours of TV a day. These figures highlight the influence of television on our children.

The numbers themselves are numbing, but then the question arises, "If kids are watching that much television, what are they *not* doing?" Many of them are not reading, exploring, exercising, playing . . . the list goes on.

So is television the enemy? Fortunately, there are many positive aspects of television. Television can introduce children to new vocabulary and experiences. It can spark new interests and hobbies for children. Television can expose children to good role models. It delivers a great deal of useful information and can actually encourage reading if books relate to a topic shown on TV.

Unfortunately, the downside of television can't be ignored. Television is a passive medium. The decreased attention span seen in children in part can be blamed on excessive TV viewing. All the problems of the world can be solved in a half-hour TV program, which doesn't reflect real life. In addition, television shows are written with action sequences planned every few seconds. Children who watch a large amount of television have more difficulty sharing in class discussion, in that TV limits language use. They also have trouble focusing on class discussions and following directions.

The question is not if your child should watch television, but how to be wise about your child's viewing habits. Here are some ideas for "unplugging" TV's negative influences:

- Limit your child's television viewing. One to two hours a day total is a good figure to begin with. Have your child read a TV guide and plan his or her viewing, instead of channel surfing.
- Be a model. Limit your watching, too, and turn off the TV if it is just being used as background noise. Let your child see you reading a book instead of watching TV.
- Watch some programs with your child, and engage your child in conversation. Ask your child to describe favorite characters. Discuss setting, plot, theme. Ask open-ended questions that require critical thinking and may have more than one answer.
- Guide your child toward quality television. Public television is a great place to start.

Sincerely,

On Parenting

Letters on parenting are supplementary letters you can send home as a service to parents. Parents appreciate being armed with information on how to raise their children. The tone of these letters is not authoritarian, but instead they read like one friend sharing ideas with another. And better parenting makes for students who function better in the classroom.

Rationale for Sending Home These Letters

Birth Order Letter. Some parents compare siblings. They may blame your instruction if you are teaching a second-born child who isn't reading as fast as the first born, for example. This letter stresses the importance of valuing each child's uniqueness.

Boredom Letter. Kids learn valuable skills when they learn to alleviate boredom. The boredom-busting skills of initiative and effort transfer to the classroom.

Choosing Clothes Letter. Children who have choices in their lives learn to be more self-directed individuals. Choosing clothes also contributes to responsible behavior. Parents will appreciate tips that make this sometimes difficult task easier.

Chores Letter. Students who have chores at home actually are better performers at school. Children who experience belonging at home by doing chores will be contributing members of the classroom as well.

Death and Grieving Letter. Should a death occur during the school year, this letter is a great resource for both teacher and parents. Children grieve differently than adults, and parents can really use information on how to help their children through the grief process.

Habits Letter. Habits are common in the early years. Parents may discuss their children's habits with you at conference time and ask for your help. This letter explains to parents what experts believe is the best approach to dealing with habits.

Hobbies Letter. Hobbies boost self-esteem and are good for the mind. Parents and children can spend quality time together with shared hobbies. This letter will give some parents the motivation to help their child pick up a hobby.

Morning Hassles Letter. If it is indeed true that the tone of the day is set by the morning routine, then both you and your students' parents would benefit from passing out this information. There are simple actions to take to make mornings at home run more smoothly, and this letter outlines them.

Nature and Children Letter. This letter is a gentle reminder that children need to spend a good amount of time outdoors and lists ways of making the most out of outdoor time.

Power Struggles Letter. They occur in the classroom, and they occur at home and anywhere else where adults and children congregate. Power struggles can be diffused by following the steps in this letter.

Sleep and Nutrition Letter. When a child has a behavior problem in the classroom, look at lack of sleep or improper nutrition as a possible cause. Better yet, send home this letter to avert some of these problems.

Birth Order

Dear Parents:

Your child is a unique human being—different in many ways from all other children. But when children in a family are different, it can be baffling, although it shouldn't be. We can thank birth order for the fact that no two siblings are exactly alike.

The family is the first place we make decisions about how to be special in the world. One child might be popular and outgoing; the other might be more reserved and artistic. This is why so many parents have said, "My second born is nothing like my oldest," or some such expression.

Much research has been done on typical responses to life according to one's position in the family. That research has produced some generalizations about how people behave, although there are many exceptions to these generalizations.

First-born children are often achievers, leaders, and helpers. They make their mark in the world by being first and best. On the flip side, they sometimes need to learn to relax and have fun. They often are perfectionistic and need to learn it is okay to make mistakes.

Second-born children, seeing that the first place is taken, choose another way to stand out. They might be social, well liked, and more relaxed. Second-born children can be less responsible than their older sibling. Second-born children need their own interests separate from the older child. They need a sounding board for their feelings and to know it's okay to feel angry and hurt sometimes.

Middle children like to maintain balance and harmony. They need lots of individual attention. Sometimes middle children see life as unfair without the privileges associated with being the oldest or youngest. It's helpful to point out a middle child's strengths and talents.

Youngest children can be charming and entertaining. Some of them, however, try to compete and try to catch up with older siblings. Young children need to be taken seriously and to be given opportunities to be responsible.

Only children can take on the roles of first-born or youngest children.

Probably the best reason for looking at the effects of birth order is to remember that children in a family can't be compared. Each child can be valued for his or her uniqueness and for the special contributions that child makes to the family. These differences play out in the classroom, and so you may have two children who perform quite differently in school. Capitalize on each child's individual assets.

Sincerely,

Boredom

Dear Parents:

"There's nothing to do!" This sentiment, expressed by every child at some point, is actually a grand invitation to one of life's great lessons: Boredom can be overcome. A little boredom can actually be a good thing.

When kids get so bored with boredom, they must find the inner resources to entertain themselves. Doing this involves using creativity, problem solving, and imagination. What results from busting boredom is a sense of accomplishment that leads to heightened feelings of self-worth. Overcoming boredom also builds a child's confidence in his or her problem-solving skills. Boredom can trigger daydreaming, which can lead to greater self-awareness. These daydreams can help children discover their deepest needs and feelings. These discoveries are not often made on the soccer field or during a piano lesson. And knowing how to combat boredom helps children tolerate waiting more effectively.

But getting children to beat boredom on their own is a challenge. Your child may stand in front of you, begging to be entertained. He or she might even get a little mad. Scolding and lecturing a child who is "crying boredom" doesn't work, but what will work is showing empathy and communicating, "I am sorry you are bored, but I'm sure you'll figure what to do about it." Your child may kick and fuss some more, but some children need to vent their feelings before they can plunge in and combat boredom quietly on their own. A bored child may try to play on your guilt, or try to make you feel sorry for him or her. It's helpful to remember there is nothing wrong with asking a child to keep occupied for a while.

A popular tool for fixing boredom is the television. Television is okay as an occasional distraction, but it's not healthy for TV to be the sole answer to boredom. You may want to limit television somewhat to encourage your child to be resourceful. Another antiboredom aid is extracurricular activities. Overscheduled children don't get the chance to learn how to initiate activities on their own. On the flip side, if your child is perpetually bored, you might want to look at adding an activity or encouraging some friendships.

Probably the best activity to suggest to a bored child is reading. Encourage the reading habit in your child, and you may never hear those two words—"I'm bored!"— again. Many children are used to being entertained. Through learning to overcome boredom, children can learn they have control over their problems.

Sincerely,

Choosing Clothes

Dear Parents:

In the classroom, I am delighted when I see students who can think for themselves and have high self-esteem. I encourage these qualities in the classroom, and you can help support them, too, by one practice at home: letting your child choose the clothes he or she will wear to school. Some of you already do this and could give other parents a list of pointers. In case your child is not setting out his or her own clothes yet, here are some tips to help you and your child get started:

- Set out clothes in the evening. This avoids morning hassles when time is of the essence. Also, children choose their clothes more quickly when they have ample time to do so.
- Start out with a choice between two outfits and work up to more independent clothing selection.
- Truly allow your child to choose. Offer an opinion, which will be received better if it's not a lecture.
- Put away out-of-season clothes to avoid that famous problem.
- Let your child wear two different colored socks if he or she wants to. (Some kids really go for this.) As long as their dress does not distract from the learning process and is in compliance with school dress requirements, let the consequences of wearing unconventional outfits regulate your child's choice of clothes. Have faith in your neighbors (and me) that we won't think you picked *that* for your child to wear.
- If your child is dressing for an important event, like Aunt Trudy's wedding, ask for your child's cooperation. Teach your child that at times we choose to wear certain clothes out of respect for other people's needs or circumstances.
- Demonstrating respect for your child's choices may lead to less rebellion. Allow your child to choose clothing within certain parameters.

Letting your child choose his or her own clothes is really an exercise in "letting go." You are giving your child power when you allow clothing choice, and you are communicating respect for your child's judgment. All this leads to your child viewing himself or herself as a capable person.

Sincerely,

Chores

Dear Parents:

Children who do chores at home achieve better in school than children who do not do chores. This is one of those research results that is hard to explain at face value. But when we look at all that chores teach a child, the idea makes a little more sense. Children who do chores learn:

To keep commitments	To organize their time
To plan ahead	To follow through
That they are skilled	That they are capable

Often, it is easier to do chores ourselves than to enlist the help of a child. When a child is given chores, parents communicate to the child that "you are an important and useful member our family. Your contributions are needed and appreciated." Parents who don't involve their children communicate that "you're not really needed here." Chores are a great opportunity for children to learn how capable they are.

Some chores that might be appropriate for your child are:

- Helping with grocery shopping
- Making his or her own sandwich
- Making the bed
- Cleaning out the inside of the car
- Taking out the garbage
- Setting the table
- Raking leaves
- Watering plants
- Straightening a drawer
- Picking up toys

Telling your child that chores are a great way to learn responsibility may not be effective. You know best what will motivate your child. One thing that doesn't work, however, is nagging and reminding. A way to get around this is to have a secret symbol, like a ribbon placed on your child's bedroom door, to remind your child that chores need to be done.

When your child does a chore, he or she will have a greater respect for all the work you do around the house. Family chores are a positive cycle that pays off for all members involved.

Sincerely,

Death and Grieving

Dear Parents:

Death is something few children have any experience with, due in part to modern technology, hospitals, and funeral homes. In addition, children grieve differently than adults. They may become quite fearful when a loved one dies and may need reassurance that they or their parents are not going to die soon. Some children have confused ideas about death that need to be sorted out. It's best to be truthful with children, without adding too many details. Children may not completely understand what has happened, but just talking about death can make it seem less mysterious.

There are some things that adults tend to say to children about death that probably are best not said:

"Grandpa has gone on a long trip." This could lead to feelings of abandonment and false hope that Grandpa will return.

"Aunt Theresa died because she was sick." Children at your child's age can't tell the difference between serious illness and common childhood illness.

"Dying is like sleeping." Children will develop a fear of taking a nap or sleeping.

"Uncle Rob has to go to the hospital for a long time." This teaches a child to learn to just forget about unpleasant things.

When in doubt as to what to say to a grieving child, listen to what the child has to say. Help your child be aware of his or her feelings. The worst thing to do when a death has occurred is to act as if nothing has happened.

As mentioned earlier, children grieve differently. Some children may seem to be coping well, while bewildered and confused on the inside. At times, the child may deny the death, or may be irritable or angry. Some children grieve in short spurts and are able to play and be seemingly happy in between. All of these reactions are part of healthy grief.

The decision of whether or not to attend the funeral can be left up to the child. It is usually the child who has been forced into attending a funeral service who is distraught. Attending a funeral can give your child a sense of completion, which can be helpful in the grieving process.

Finally, a great way to take care of your child during a difficult time such as this is by taking care of yourself as well. Your child will look to you for cues on the whole grieving process. This is a great opportunity for you and your child to give each other comfort and for you to teach your child about death as a part of life.

Sincerely,

Habits

Dear Parents:

At this age, your child is experiencing newness and changes that come in the primary years: new school experiences, new friends, and maybe some other "new"s in your family situation, such as a new house or a new sibling. This newness can be exciting but also can be a period of stress for your youngster. That is why your child may try out a few habits that, depending on what they are, may or may not annoy you. Habits such as nail biting, hair twirling, or feet tapping may not be cute, but they most often are temporary.

Unfortunately, the more parents beg, nag, threaten, or cajole a child into giving up a habit, the greater momentum the habit develops. Stopping a habit is up to the child. Some children can get caught up in negative attention they get from a habit, and that attention may even make the habit stronger. What you can do is communicate that you love your child exactly as he or she is. You can offer suggestions for relieving tension, such as deep breathing. You can offer an object, such as a rubber ball, for your child to squeeze in times of stress. If a habit is particularly distasteful, as in nose picking, you may want to tell your child you will need to leave the room because of it. This approach eliminates negative attention and could be quite effective. Encouraging your child to share feelings as a way to relieve stress is another habit-busting technique.

There is a difference between habits and tics, which are physical in nature and not caused by stress. Tics fall into two categories: motor (blinking of the eyes or shaking one's head) and vocal (clearing the throat or coughing). Tics are not used to relieve tension because they are not under the child's direct control. Tics are surprisingly common—one child in eight will develop a tic. It's best to relax about tics, because they come and go, with most disappearing after a few weeks or months. If a tic persists or is especially troublesome, the child should be seen by a doctor who may prescribe medication.

We all have ways of relieving tension. Children with habits have just found socially less appropriate ways to channel their energy. Some habits die out due to comments made by friends. But until a habit does fizzle, it's best for the parent to remember, "This, too, shall pass!"

Sincerely,

Hobbies

Dear Parents:

Self-esteem is not something we can give a child, but it can be nurtured in several ways. One road toward increased feelings of self-worth is having a hobby. Children who have hobbies are less likely to be involved in unhealthy pursuits. Having a hobby gives children yet another thing that is special about them.

Hobbies stem from your child's natural interests and cannot be forced. Therefore, be an advocate for your child's interests. If your child loves dogs, take your child to the library to do research, go to dog shows with your child, and perhaps have a dog as a pet. Supporting your child in his or her hobby communicates that you respect your child's choices and desires. Some hobbies your child might enjoy at this age are:

Collecting. Shells and rocks are popular items to collect because they are easily obtained. Other items kids like to collect are dolls, stamps (good for history and geography), toy cars, comic books, and trading cards. Teach your child that you don't need to spend money to collect. In fact, additions to collections can be more meaningful when traded for or received from a relative.

Model making. Children used to make more models than they do today, and a decrease in scores of spatial ability (involving the ability to imagine something and build it) is evidence of that trend. Bring back modeling with your child if he or she is interested in cars, airplanes, or structures.

Pet care. Children are drawn to animals, which makes pet care a popular hobby for children. For children to have ownership of this hobby, they need to be given some if not most of the responsibility for the animal's care. If your child is caring for an animal full time, however, make sure you give your child periodic breaks from that great responsibility.

Team sports. Sports can teach a child so much about cooperation, problem solving, and being a good sport. Before your child joins a team, make sure he or she is aware of the commitment involved in being part of a team. Hold off on money invested in a new sport, as well as any other hobby, until you are sure of your child's commitment.

Having a hobby yourself will encourage your child to find one, too. Finding a hobby that's right for your child may require trial and error. Once a good match is found, that hobby will help your child make his or her mark in the world.

Sincerely,

Morning Hassles

Dear Parents:

It's frightening sometimes to think the tone for the day is set in the morning routine. Getting children off to school, happy and on time, can be a Herculean feat. Morning preparations can run more smoothly and can actually be a special time of the day. Here are some suggestions:

Get ready for morning the night before. Have your child decide what to wear, put together any papers needed for school, and do as many other preparations as possible the night before. Squeeze in getting ready for school between brushing teeth and story time, perhaps. This is the best way to relieve morning stress.

Teach your child to use an alarm clock. Children at your child's age can learn to set a clock and let it wake them in the morning. Together, you and your child can decide how much time is needed in the morning. Set the alarm according to the time you both have budgeted.

Use humor. By keeping things light in the morning, you invite cooperation. Also, making a game out of some tasks can be effective. (Make a race out of putting on socks and shoes.)

Television doesn't go on until a child is ready to go out the door. You may need to use this rule if your child gets mesmerized by TV. It also can be an incentive for your child to get ready for school quickly.

Allow your child to experience consequences. We have a policy for dealing with tardiness at our school. If your child is choosing to dawdle in the morning and you are doing all you can do to get him or her moving, please write me a note. I will explain our school's policy to your child and will apply the consequences if tardiness continues.

It's best, however, if the problem can be solved at home. Getting ready for school is a challenge your child will face for many years to come with many other teachers. Teaching your child to be responsible and to manage time is a great gift.

Sincerely,

Letter 6.9

Nature and Children

Dear Parents:

With Americans spending more than 95% of their lives indoors, it's no wonder children have less opportunities to dig holes, jump in puddles, climb trees, sail boats down streams, and many other activities that involve nature. On top of that, by the year 2000, more than 90% of the American population will live in urban areas. There is a historic trend that is removing children farther and farther from wild places, denying many children the opportunity to get to know the great outdoors. When children do go outdoors, it is often to play in the cement jungles we call playgrounds. These areas allow kids to run around and let off steam, but they don't allow children to make discoveries that come from interacting with nature.

A connection to nature is an important part of healthy child development. Children are naturally attracted to the out-of-doors, but without nurturing, that attraction decreases with age. To fail to capitalize on a young child's affinity for nature is to deny that child a crucial part of growing up. Memories from childhood of times spent outdoors are carried into adulthood, where they are cherished. To create those memories with your child, you can:

Provide the setting. Budget outdoor time into your child's daily routine, if you don't do so already. Nature really can be found anywhere, so set out with your child to discover it. It's ideal if children can have a place outdoors to explore and make special places. This can be your backyard, the park, or any other safe outdoor setting. Children like to make secret, enclosed places where they can have a broad view of what is going on around them. A child's idea of a good time in nature is the small space directly in front of him or her, where the worms roam and the weeds sprout. It is important for children to feel ownership of their special places. If possible, set aside part of your yard as a natural area, and don't tidy it up.

Go on long walks. Go outdoors as much as possible. While on these walks, encourage your child to use all five senses. For children to keep a sense of wonder, it helps if at least one encouraging adult nurtures a love of nature throughout the child's life. Your job as nature guide on these walks is not to name everything you see, but to focus on the beauty and wonder of nature. Sometimes when children ask, "What's that?" they really want to know more than just the name of the object. So instead of just providing a name, ask further questions like "Why do you think the lizard is that color?" or "What is that butterfly doing?" When faced with a question you don't know the answer to, admit it and suggest that you and your child find the answer together.

By making a connection with nature, children can gain a sense of self-worth. Children can also learn to appreciate the beauty of nature. Being in nature allows children to make sense of their world and to understand their place in it.

Sincerely,

Power Struggles

Dear Parents:

It's hard to see power struggles with your child as a normal, healthy part of your child's development. But through power struggles, a child is taking one more step toward independence. Power struggles are part of a child's life, but what an adult does with these struggles makes all the difference. An adult may want to win during a power struggle, but in true power struggles no one is the winner. The best an adult can hope for is to diffuse the struggle. This can be done by:

- Conveying authority in a cool manner. Once your cheeks get red, you're into a power struggle. Remember, power struggles take no prisoners. Breathe deeply, close your eyes for a minute, do whatever it takes to lift yourself above the battlefield.
- Find a way to agree with your child on some point. If you can't say yes now to your child's request, tell your child when the answer might be yes.
- Is your child using power to get attention? If so, look for ways to provide positive attention to your child.
- Pick your battles. Focus on issues that are important to your child's well-being.
- Be sensitive to struggles when you and your child are feeling tired or rushed.
- Have a few iron-clad rules that are never broken.
- Evaluate your own need for power. Is your child learning from a master?

On the bright side, children who engage in power struggles often have good leadership qualities. They are children who tend to be able to think for themselves. Finding ways to diffuse power struggles without squelching your child's assertiveness is a tricky balance. Knowing your child can help you find creative ways to stop power struggles before they start.

Sincerely,

Sleep and Nutrition

Dear Parents:

"Eat a good breakfast and get plenty of sleep the night before." You may remember receiving this advice from a teacher before taking a big test in school. But this is actually good advice for every student for every day of school. A lack of proper rest or poor nutrition leads to a host of problems in the classroom, all of which can be avoided by healthier habits.

Nutrition and learning. Children who are well nourished have energy that carries them through all the demands of a school day: classroom assignments, friendships, physical activities, and other challenges. Children who eat nutritiously have a greater attention span than their less healthy counterparts. They are able to concentrate and learn more as a result. The best place to start each day is with a nutritious breakfast, which the U.S. Department of Agriculture describes as juice or fruit, bread or cereal, milk, and meat or meat substitute (eggs, fish, cheese).

A nutritious lunch is also crucial to carry your child through the second half of the school day. Protein and iron should be included in your child's diet for healthy brain development and functioning. Protein can be found in meat, fish, dairy products, fowl, peas, beans, and nuts. Iron can be found in dark green leafy vegetables, eggs, meats, and raisins. Iron deficiency anemia can lead to inattention and some learning disabilities.

Sleep and learning. A lack of sleep can produce children who are irritable, cranky, sluggish, and unfocused. These qualities interfere with the learning process. If your child displays any of these characteristics, it's a relief to know that providing your child with more time to sleep may help these problems disappear. In fact, whenever a new behavioral problem pops up with your child, look to a lack of sleep first as a possible cause of the problem.

To discover how much sleep your child needs, you will need a week (perhaps on vacation) where you let your child sleep as long as he or she needs. This will give a good indication of the number of hours of sleep your child's body requires. Typical five-year-old children need between 11 and 12 hours a sleep at night, and six- to eight-year-old children need 10 ¼ to 10 ¾ hours of sleep, although sleep needs do vary among children. If your child is staying up late, you might want to wake him or her up 15 minutes earlier each day for a few days. The sleep deprivation that will result will help your child fall asleep sooner at night.

Sincerely,

7

On Children's Social Skills

This is an area where teachers need all the help they can get. Social skills instruction must be supported at home to be effective. These letters explain what the teacher is doing to foster each social skill and what parents can do at home to reinforce the skills.

Rationale for Sending Home These Letters

Being a Good Sport Letter. Poor sportsmanship causes a host of problems in the classroom. Techniques for developing good sportsmanship are listed in this letter.

Dealing With Conflict Letter. Conflict is both a natural part of life and a contributor to disruptions in the classroom. When parents help their children with conflict at home, those children are more able to handle conflict at school.

Dealing With Frustration Letter. Children learn by being able to pull out of a frustration tailspin. Teaching children to persevere is one of the best gifts we can give children. Parents will see frustration as a learning opportunity for their children.

Dealing With Peer Pressure Letter. Parents of children in the early years are just beginning to see the power friends have over their children. This letter conveys how to offer a child healthy independence while still remaining influential in the child's life.

Diversity Letter. This letter presents a case for multicultural education. Diversity is a rarely discussed subject, but accepting diversity is an important developmental task.

Goal Setting Letter. Specific strategies for setting goals are listed in this letter. When parents, teacher, and students set goals together, great things can be accomplished.

Intrinsic Motivation Letter. Successful learners are motivated from the inside. It may surprise some parents to know that rewards and punishments do not motivate students to achieve. This letter makes a case for guiding children to be internally directed.

Making Friends Letter. Friendships greatly influence a child's attitude toward school. In addition, some parents are unfamiliar with the normal ups and downs of childhood friendships. This letter helps parents support their children's friendships.

Negotiating Letter. Parents can identify where their child is on a negotiation skills continuum and can learn ways to encourage negotiation through this letter.

Organization Letter. Tips for helping children become more organized are given in this letter. An organized child is a more successful student.

Problem Solving Letter. Parents are given specific steps for helping their children solve problems in this letter. Student problem solving reduces disruptions in the classroom and transfers to academic areas as well.

Responsibility Letter. Responsibility cannot be taught by the teacher alone. Send out this letter to enlist help from parents.

Risk Taking Letter. Students who take risks learn more. Risk taking does not come naturally to all students, and this letter can help parents encourage healthy risk taking in their children.

Letter 7.1

Being a Good Sport

Dear Parents:

Dealing with losing and winning, whether at a board game or an athletic event, is part of learning to be a good sport. Children vary in their sportsmanship abilities, and some children benefit from instruction on handling the outcomes of competitions.

WHAT WE ARE DOING AT SCHOOL

The children are taught to do the following:

1. End a game positively. (Say "congratulations," shake hands, compliment the other player or team, ask for a rematch. All comments are encouraged to be sincere. The students are also taught to watch their body language to make sure their movements and gestures match what they are saying.)
2. Work with others to put materials or equipment away.
3. Leave the game on the playing field (and no "Monday morning quarterbacking").

HOW HOME AND SCHOOL CAN WORK TOGETHER

When playing games or sports at home, insist on the behaviors listed above. In addition, take time to teach your child about:

- Winning—explain the problems with gloating and how to be a gracious winner.
- Losing—teach your child that someone usually has to lose in a game or sports competition. Help your child find ways to find comfort after a loss, such as doing a favorite activity or helping another person.

Children whose whole self-concept gets wrapped up in a competition need to be reminded that, win or lose, they are still valued and loved.

Sincerely,

Dealing With Conflict

Dear Parents:

Conflict is a natural part of life and actually is fertile ground for learning. Since conflict is natural, we don't need to fear it, but rather we should be ready to resolve it when it arises.

Children, like adults, face conflict in one of three ways:

1. *Passively.* "Good kids" often react this way. When a battle begins, passive children will put the needs of others before their own to keep the peace. Whereas this may stop the conflict, it is not a healthy way to react to conflict with regularity.
2. *Aggressively.* Children who act aggressively may shout, bully, or act in such a way as to intimidate the other person. Again, this is not a healthy response. Aggressive children need guidance to learn to settle disputes calmly.
3. *Assertively.* This is the ideal method for handling conflict. Children who act assertively defend themselves while still respecting the other party or parties involved.

WHAT WE ARE DOING AT SCHOOL

When conflict arises, both parties will be asked to step aside to mediate. Each child will have a chance to tell his or her side of the story without interruption. Finger-pointing will be discouraged, and "I-messages" encouraged (for example, "I felt embarrassed when you made fun of my name"). Each child will be asked to restate what the other child said. Solutions will be offered by both parties, and together the children will find one or two that they want to try.

HOW HOME AND SCHOOL CAN WORK TOGETHER

The following skills and behaviors that help with resolving conflicts are effectively taught at home:

- Using I-messages (Instead of saying, "You made me so mad," teach your child to say, "I felt mad when . . .")
- Restating other people's words
- Recognizing and understanding feelings
- Actively listening
- Appreciating differences in other people

Sincerely,

Dealing With Frustration

Dear Parents:

When children launch into a tailspin of frustration, it's our job as adults to guide them out of it. However, we needn't jump in and do all the work of recovering equilibrium. Experiencing frustration can be a transformative experience, one children shouldn't be denied now and then. The most important lesson for a child to learn concerning frustration is how to get past the frustration itself. When your child is able to do this, he or she is using coping mechanisms that will last a lifetime.

WHAT WE ARE DOING AT SCHOOL

When your child is visibly frustrated, I might use any or all of the following approaches:

- Ask your child to explain what the problem is.
- Ask your child what steps can be taken to make things better.
- Make suggestions for making things better.
- Ask your child if he or she needs to step away from the task for a while.
- Stay away from your child and let him or her have some space to work things out.
- Remind your child that everyone makes mistakes and that there would be no need for school if people were born perfect.

When we are working on art projects, at times students become frustrated with their work. I encourage the students to continue with the piece they are working on, rather than scrapping the project. This helps those students whose art will never be perfect enough for them. It teaches children to solve problems in the context of art. Whenever a child breaks through frustration and accomplishes a task, I will point out to the child the merit of sticking with something even when the going gets tough.

HOW HOME AND SCHOOL CAN WORK TOGETHER

Along with the approaches listed above, you can make an extra effort to communicate that mistakes are part of the learning process. Try some relaxation techniques (deep breathing, relaxing muscles) with your child that he or she could use when frustrated. Tell stories of people who have persevered through difficulties. Most of all, model overcoming your own frustration to your child.

Sincerely,

Dealing With Peer Pressure

Dear Parents:

Peer pressure is a challenge usually associated with adolescence, but its roots are in the early years. If you've experienced your child dropping your hand when you get near the classroom, where it used to be clasped tight around yours, you've experienced your child's first struggles with peer pressure. Your child is branching out, and this step toward independence is all part of normal, healthy development.

WHAT WE ARE DOING AT SCHOOL

I am concerned with peer pressure at school because it can lead children to misbehavior and using poor judgment. Therefore, I guide children to think of the consequences of their behaviors whenever appropriate. Children who have interests, hobbies, and special talents are less likely to give in to the pressures of others. So the best way I can help with peer pressure is by offering a rich curriculum and a stimulating school day to your child. I lead my students toward self-respect by asking their opinions, having faith in their abilities, and treating their thoughts and actions as important contributions to our classroom. We also discuss from time to time how daring to be different for the right reasons is something to aspire to.

HOW HOME AND SCHOOL CAN WORK TOGETHER

When it comes right down to it, parents are the determining factor in a child's ability to resist pressure. Some ideas on helping a young child with peer pressure are:

- Help your child to feel unconditionally loved.
- Show understanding of your child's desire to be part of a group.
- Don't sweat the small stuff. Save your energy for bigger battles that need your credibility and influence.
- Teach your child to give reasons for not going along with pressure to do something. Help your child learn how to suggest another activity when pressured to do something he or she doesn't want to do.
- Role-play with your child situations that require your child to say no.
- Listen to your child every day.

Parents sometimes feel as though they are losing influence with their children as they grow older and peers become more of a force in their lives. But your child still wants and needs your guidance, and your opinions still really do matter.

Sincerely,

Letter 7.5

Diversity

Dear Parents:

There are hundreds of different cultures in the United States. This diversity is our strength. In addition, what's referred to now as minority cultures will make up half of America's population by the middle of the next century. The change in our country's cultural balance has made some people nervous. This apprehension is partly due to fear of the unknown, which leads some to mistrust the benefits of a diverse society.

WHAT WE ARE DOING AT SCHOOL

Our classroom goal is to conquer any fear by bringing the unknown into the known. Your child will receive information about diversity from television, books, toys, advertising, and the news media. This information may or may not portray an acceptance of diversity. Your child will learn understanding of diversity in the classroom by being exposed to different cultures through books, activities, and discussions, as well as interactions with other students. When children learn about other cultures, they grow in understanding of their own lives as well.

Children can be uncomfortable around others who are different. By educating my students about differences in culture, any fear will be replaced with curiosity, tolerance, and acceptance.

HOW HOME AND SCHOOL CAN WORK TOGETHER

Start by evaluating your acceptance of diversity. Examine what you say about ethnic foods, ethnic dress, certain neighborhoods, holidays, and features considered attractive in a person. The following are some other ways to help your child:

- Discuss with your child how other cultures have influenced and are a part of your lives.
- Talk about diversity with your child before he or she is negatively influenced by outside sources.
- Give your child opportunities to experience diversity firsthand.
- Model an acceptance of all cultures.

Developmentally, children go through periods of favoring playmates who are similar to themselves. These preferences wax and wane, and decrease with age, as children let go of racial preferences. With our guidance, your child will appreciate diversity and all it has to offer.

Sincerely,

Goal Setting

Dear Parents:

Students who set goals take greater responsibility for their learning. Therefore, my students set goals in our classroom. But goal setting doesn't have to stop there. You can help your child set goals by following these steps:

1. Follow your child's lead. Set goals with your child only if he or she is truly interested in doing so. Goals should be self-initiated and self-directed.
2. Encourage your child. Children who are used to following adult guidance may have difficulty thinking for themselves of something they'd like to learn or achieve.
3. Help your child choose a goal that is realistic. Consider the actual task and the amount of time your child has allotted for the goal. If your child's goal is unreasonable, you can step in and help your child reshape the goal.
4. Help your child decide what steps are necessary to complete the goal. List the steps somewhere as a reminder.
5. Watch your child mark off the steps as they are completed.
6. When the goal is met, teach your child how to reward himself or herself.

The more you can put the whole goal-setting process in your child's hands, the more intrinsically rewarding the experience will be. Your child's goal could be academic (learning math facts or reading a number of books), behavioral (not biting nails or not hitting little brother), or social (asking someone to play at school or giving compliments). Your child will experience the most success with small goals that have steps and can be met in a short time period.

Through meeting a goal, your child will want to set another one and yet another one. Meeting the particular goal is important, but the goal-setting process is where the real learning takes place.

Sincerely,

Intrinsic Motivation

Dear Parents:

Children can be led to do a task from the outside (rewards or punishments) or from inside (having a true desire to do something). I didn't use the word *motivate,* because truly we can't motivate another person. What we can do is manipulate someone into doing what we want, but this is not motivation. Motivation comes from inside a person, and whereas we can't motivate other people, we can create a motivating environment by modeling and encouragement. Inner, or *intrinsic,* motivation is a great predictor of future school success and therefore is something I foster in the classroom.

WHAT WE ARE DOING AT SCHOOL

Rewards and punishments are not used to encourage children in the classroom. Punishment lasts only as long as the adult is in the room. Rewards cause a child to become less interested in whatever it was the adult wanted the child to do. Both rewards and punishments are controlling and thus are likely to be negative in the long run. I do the following to help children find intrinsic motivation:

- Provide lessons that are meaningful to students' lives. Children are naturally curious and motivated. When a lesson applies to their own lives and interests, children find it in themselves to be motivated.
- Provide choices throughout the day. Having choices gives children a feeling of control, rather than being controlled. This feeling leads to greater motivation.
- Give positive feedback, not meaningless praise. The goal is for children to want to achieve for themselves, not just to please me. I will direct them to see the positive in whatever they do.

HOW HOME AND SCHOOL CAN WORK TOGETHER

Look at how often you give your child a "goody" for doing something well. Watch for your child saying either "What do I get if I . . . ?" or "What will happen if I . . . ?" These are signs that your child is being directed by something other than his or her own inner controls. Help your child to see the relevance or purpose of a task. For example, explain how taking out the trash really helps the whole family. It may sound hokey, but enlist your child's help in developing family rules. Your child is much more likely to follow them, and for all the right reasons, if he or she has had a hand in creating them.

Sincerely,

Making Friends

Dear Parents:

By now, your child has probably come home with stories of friendships won, lost, and won again on the school playground. Your child's relationships with classmates will have a big impact on how your child perceives school this year. The process of friendship development can be exciting, but it is also frequently exhausting. Some friendship-making skills from *Skillstreaming the Elementary School Child,* published by the Research Press Company in 1984, that you may want to work on with your child are as follows:

- Introducing oneself
- Beginning a conversation
- Ending a conversation
- Joining in
- Offering to help a classmate
- Giving a compliment
- Accepting a compliment
- Suggesting an activity
- Sharing
- Apologizing

Pick any skill you would like to work on with your child, and break it up into tiny steps. Be absolutely specific. For example, if you would like to work with your child on the skill of joining in, speak about how to recognize a group he or she would like to join. Suggest how to approach a group of friends ("Do you run and burst in, or do you walk up calmly and say to your friends, 'What are you doing?' "). Tell your child joining in does not mean immediately trying to get the group to do what he or she wants to do. Finally, talk about how to be a good group member once the child is in the group (smiling, sharing, taking turns). Then, the two of you can act out how to positively join in. This is the fun part. We take for granted that such friendship skills develop naturally, but at times they need explicit instruction.

Often, the child who struggles with making and keeping friends has difficulty in one or more of the areas listed above. Children at your child's age prefer predictability and like to be around other kids who follow social norms and who are cooperative. Every now and then, however, one child will hook up with another child with less developed social skills. Whereas you can't control who your child is attracted to, you can help your child handle the outcomes of such a friendship. Be there as a guide for your child, listening and offering suggestions. Usually, ill-fated unions between classmates fizzle away quickly on their own, as the children move on to find more suitable companions.

One final idea to remember: It is easy to get caught up in the drama of childhood friendships. It is our job as adults to be the voices of reason and to model rational problem solving when friendship crises pop up.

Sincerely,

Negotiating

Dear Parents:

Does your child have leadership potential? One sign of this is the ability to negotiate in the early years. Whereas true negotiation skills don't bloom until ages 8 through 11, some children show early negotiation ability, and most children can learn this ability if not present. Children usually pass through four stages of negotiation skill.

1. *Negotiation through force.* This stage is characterized by hitting, bullying, pushing, or yelling. Many preschool age children are at this stage.
2. *"You say to-may-to, I say to-mah-to."* At this stage where many kindergarten students find themselves, children know they have different opinions but can't see the other person's side of the story.
3. *Let's make a deal.* Children try to influence the other person into going along with them. Deal making and bargaining are used in this stage. Children as young as kindergarten age can be taught techniques for this level of negotiation.
4. *True negotiation.* Children at this stage of negotiation have mutual respect and can work out solutions that are good for all parties involved.

WHAT WE ARE DOING AT SCHOOL

Children are encouraged to negotiate by following these steps:

- When a disagreement arises, tell how you feel about the problem.
- Ask the other person to tell how he or she feels.
- Listen without interrupting.
- Make a suggestion that will satisfy both parties.

HOW HOME AND SCHOOL CAN WORK TOGETHER

Encourage negotiation in your family by following the steps listed above. Point out successful negotiation when you see it, either in real life or on television. Finally, keep in mind that your child may not be developmentally ready for a certain level of negotiation. What you can do now is plant the seeds for future success.

Sincerely,

Letter 7.10

Organization

Dear Parents:

Some children seem born with it, others do not. But organizational skill can be taught to those missing the "orderly gene." Additionally, some children are quite comfortable with chaos while their parents are tearing their hair out. The important thing is to teach each child enough organization for success in school and at home.

WHAT WE ARE DOING AT SCHOOL

Your child's special spaces at school are expected to be organized. When an area becomes disheveled, the child will be asked to put it back in order. Some children need very specific directions as to how to accomplish this, and I provide that training. I take nothing for granted and break down the process of organizing into very small, manageable steps. Also, we never let areas get to the point where the task of cleaning would be monumental.

I don't do for children what they can do for themselves. Children who have adults who clean up after them miss the opportunity to develop organizational skills.

HOW HOME AND SCHOOL CAN WORK TOGETHER

Make your child in charge of a small area at home to start, if your child isn't already. Perhaps start with your child's desk or bookshelf. Train your child to know what is organized (pencils in the pencil cup, papers in a stack, books with spines facing outward). Once your child has that area under control, branch out to other areas.

Keeping a calendar is a good organizational tool. Having a central family calendar or a personal calendar can help your child anticipate upcoming dates and events. It's best for anyone to refer to just one calendar, organizational experts say.

Having well-defined routines at home helps with organization. Children who are raised in an orderly environment absorb it through the pores. Have a routine where you look at any schoolwork or papers from school, do with them whatever is necessary (sign the permission slip, hang the masterpiece on the refrigerator, etc.), and put the items going back to school in a consistent place so they can be found easily in the morning.

Again, sometimes it may seem easier to do things for children, such as tidying their room or picking up after them, but this may be counterproductive in the long run. You wouldn't do your child's homework for him or her, so don't deny your child the learning experience of organizing.

Sincerely,

Problem Solving

Dear Parents:

Children in the early years are faced with a number of problems in a typical day. Learning to solve them is a desirable skill to teach children. Solving problems involves critical thinking, which carries over into academic areas as well.

WHAT WE ARE DOING AT SCHOOL

My students are taught some steps to follow when faced with a problem:

1. Describe the problem.
2. Give the problem some thought. (What caused it? Who is involved? What can be done?)
3. Look at both sides of the problem. (Consider the consequences. Ask "What would happen if . . . ?")
4. Decide on a solution and follow it.
5. Decide if the solution was a good one.

In our classroom, we view problems as opportunities to learn. Helping your child solve problems increases his or her independence. Capable children solve problems effectively.

HOW HOME AND SCHOOL CAN WORK TOGETHER

You can support problem solving at home by using the steps listed above with your child. In addition, you can help by giving your child space to solve his or her own problems wherever possible.

Acknowledge when you see your child effectively solving a problem and label it as such. When you allow your child to solve problems, you are communicating your faith in his or her abilities and competence.

Sincerely,

Responsibility

Dear Parents:

It has been said that 90% of a person's habits and attitudes are in place by age 12. With that in mind, the time to encourage responsibility in your child is now. Unfortunately, we can't "give" responsibility to a child, but we can give them opportunities to learn and practice it. Responsibility grows out of an urge to contribute. To be responsible requires a healthy degree of self-esteem and independence. Children who feel significant and capable are responsible as a by-product of those characteristics. Finally, a person can be responsible when he or she is able to show concern, or has empathy, for others.

WHAT WE ARE DOING AT SCHOOL

Each member of the class is reminded often that he or she is an important, contributing member. Since responsibility thrives in environments that offer choices, opportunities for your child to make choices in the classroom are offered. Classroom jobs let children practice responsibility. We also talk often about feelings to help children develop empathy, which helps children to be responsible.

HOW HOME AND SCHOOL CAN WORK TOGETHER

Look for ways your child can contribute at home. Chores are an excellent way for a child to practice responsibility. For chores to be effective, the child must know why he or she is doing them: to make a contribution to your family.

Give your child a voice in your family. Allowing your child some influence leads to greater responsibility. Point out verbally when your child has been responsible. Talk through actions you do that require responsibility and label them as such.

We teach responsibility because it is one of those behaviors that is associated with higher achievement and happier people. It takes time to teach responsibility, but that time pays great dividends in the future.

Sincerely,

Letter 7.13

Risk Taking

Dear Parents:

There is dangerous risk taking and healthy risk taking. Dangerous risks often involve physical challenges, whereas healthy risks can be social, emotional, or academic in nature. Risk taking in the classroom centers on healthy risks: risks that lead to greater learning in your child.

WHAT WE ARE DOING AT SCHOOL

Your child is never told that he or she is wrong in the classroom. When your child gives an incorrect answer to a question, every attempt will be made to find something right in that answer. For example, if your child says Abraham Lincoln was the first president, I will not say, "That's wrong." What I will say is, "Abraham Lincoln was a president, and a very important one, but he was not our first president." This response offers respect for the child and encourages the child to try again.

I communicate respect to your child by not yelling, threatening, demeaning, or using any other punitive behaviors. This atmosphere of respect helps your child feel safe. Sarcasm and ridicule are not accepted in our room. We have as a class rule: "Never hurt anyone on the outside or the inside." This promotes the students' respect for each other. Helping your child feel comfortable with who she or he is makes your child feel safe.

Children are more likely to think more creatively and offer more opinions when they are confident they will be accepted for their uniqueness.

HOW HOME AND SCHOOL CAN WORK TOGETHER

Some children are born with initiative and others need encouragement. If your child is reluctant to try new things, try to provide the safest situation possible. Some children will still have difficulty and may need to set healthy risk taking or showing initiative as a personal goal.

When your child tries something new that is difficult, point it out. Talk about the merits of trying new things. Risk taking has a snowball effect: The more risks your child takes, the easier it becomes to take risks.

Sincerely,

On How Children Learn

Thanks to research, many strides have been made in discovering how children learn. Sharing this information with parents helps them to understand why you do what you do in the classroom. These letters help to make sense out of such concepts as constructing knowledge and emotional intelligence. These letters will both fascinate and educate parents, as well as strengthen your partnership.

Rationale for Sending Home These Letters

Active Versus Passive Learning Letter. Your students' parents may remember the days of dittos and "drill and kill," which have their place but are only part of the whole picture. We know now that children learn more when actively involved in educational pursuits. Use this letter to explain the benefits of active learning.

The Arts and Children Letter. This letter outlines the gains children make when educated through the arts and about the arts.

Constructing Knowledge Letter. The concept is still relatively new that children make meaning from activities that are connected to prior experiences. This letter enlightens parents on this exciting concept.

Cooking Letter. This letter outlines all that can be learned in the kitchen. It presents the case for hands-on learning.

Emotions and Learning Letter. Emotional development is an important part of educating the whole child. By sending out this letter, you are communicating the importance of emotions in learning.

Expectations Letter. The expectations teachers and parents have for children are determining factors in their success. This letter shows how to set high, but reachable, expectations for children.

Integrated Curriculum Letter. Most parents were educated with separate subjects, such as reading, math, and science. Send home this letter to explain how and why you integrate subject matter.

Learning Through Play Letter. Play is a misunderstood phenomenon. Many parents need to be shown the value of play and all that can be learned through activities such as block building.

Multiple Intelligences Letter. Children have different ways of "knowing" or being smart. This letter outlines multiple intelligences and introduces parents to the concept that intelligence cannot be summed up by a fixed number.

Music and Learning Letter. Parents will appreciate receiving information on how children learn through music. This letter shows the correlations between music and greater learning.

Reading Aloud to Your Child Letter. Parents are most commonly enlisted to help by reading nightly with their child. This letter contains tips for making the most of the shared reading experience.

Letter 8.1

Active Versus Passive Learning

Dear Parents:

The Chinese proverb "When I hear, I forget. When I see, I remember. When I do, I understand" sums up how children learn in my classroom. The goal is for students to be active, not passive, in all learning experiences. When students are actively engaged in a lesson, greater learning occurs. Activity takes many forms in our classroom:

Practice sheets are rarely used. If you had to change a tire in the rain, which you had never done before, you would not learn how to change one by completing a few dittos on the side of the road before reaching for a wrench. After looking at the manual, you would dive in with both hands and learn how to change a tire by doing. Practice sheets by themselves are often not meaningful for children, and therefore the information is difficult to store in the brain. In this way, practice sheets may actually slow down the learning process. If I want your child to learn the concept of measuring liquids, we will measure or cook something as opposed to simply completing a meaningless ditto with pictures of cups with liquid in them. Your child will be taught how to complete practice sheets, but they will take up a small part of the school day.

Whole group time is carefully planned. A minimum amount of time is spent lecturing, repeating directions, answering questions over and over, and in-class discussions that ramble. When we are working as a whole class, I make an effort to engage all students in what we are doing. Students who are asked to participate in the group actually start to approach me more often to contribute, making for a positive cycle of active participation.

Manipulatives are aplenty. Your child's growing brain needs concrete objects at this age to help with abstract math ideas. Your child will actually be able to perform higher math tasks with the help of manipulatives. Anyone who has ever watched a child knows how children like to touch things. Therefore, if we are studying the ocean, shells and other ocean objects will be available for learning through touching.

All children are expected to be busy. Although choices are offered throughout the day, the choice of doing nothing is not an option. I communicate with my voice to the children that they need to be learning at all times.

Learning activities are meaningful. Students are much more likely to actively participate when they are interested in the topic at hand. Lessons that build on what the students already know and that are important to them are the most powerful lessons of all.

Sincerely,

The Arts and Children

Dear Parents:

Visual arts, music, dance, and drama are the components of art education. Art is often seen as an expendable in school: fluff that's fun but not necessary in the education of children. I see art not only as enriching children's lives but as great food for intellectual development as well.

THE ARTS AND ACADEMIC DEVELOPMENT

Art is a language of its own, and communicating in any language involves skills such as reasoning, inventing, creating, and problem solving. Art is a way of expressing what is happening in a child's mind and therefore reflects a child's development. It is a highly symbolic activity, which requires children to create or recall an experience in their minds and organize and express that experience using symbols. Children can also demonstrate what they've learned through art.

THE ARTS AND EMOTIONAL DEVELOPMENT

Through art, children are able to communicate their feelings and emotions. Self-awareness is a big step toward emotional well-being, and children really come to know themselves and their thoughts and feelings through the arts. Art is a vehicle for discovering values and making decisions about one's life.

Children can also learn much by appreciating works of art. You can guide your child toward art appreciation in the following ways:

- Expose your child to a variety of art styles. With exposure, children come to know and appreciate more varying styles of art.
- Take time occasionally to focus on one genre of art, like impressionist paintings or modern dance. Such focus tends to increase a child's positive feelings toward a particular style, and it opens that child up to other works of art within that genre.
- Don't ignore the abstract. Children often show a preference for abstract art over more realistic styles.
- Share your perspectives. The conversations you have about art with your child will richly contribute to both of your lives.

Sincerely,

Constructing Knowledge

Dear Parents:

I'd love to take credit for teaching my students all they have learned so far this year, but I can't. What I have done is to create an environment for learning and provided learning cues, but the children have actually constructed their own knowledge within themselves. How a student learns something is a complex process that involves a student taking what he or she already knows and altering or adding to it with new information. The process of combining known information with new information creates feelings of contradiction that force a child to change his or her thinking to fit new understanding.

It would be so much easier if I could pour information into your child's brain, like using a pitcher to fill a glass of water. But since this is not possible, I have to set up a learning atmosphere where students can find meaning by constructing knowledge. I do that in the following ways:

- What is meaningful to my students is worth pursuing. The children's interests drive many of our learning activities. When a student is interested in a topic, greater learning is more likely to occur.
- My students are viewed as thinkers with valuable opinions. They have ideas about the world that are constantly being refined by new information. Students are never told they are wrong. All attempts are made to honor students' responses by looking for something that is correct in their responses.
- Our room is rich with real-life materials and manipulatives. Children learn by doing, and in our class the students have plenty of opportunities to do.
- Children have choices throughout the day, which leads to greater motivation. They also have a say in how our classroom operates. When children have a hand in deciding classroom rules and procedures, they are much more likely to follow them.
- Children have plenty of opportunities to work with others to learn more about the world and the people in it. My students learn from exchanging ideas with each other.

These practices do not imply that I don't directly teach my students. There are many specific skills that students need help incorporating into their minds, skills that don't come naturally. With a combination of direct teaching of skills, while setting up an atmosphere for learning, your child can take wings and learn at his or her potential.

Sincerely,

Cooking

Dear Parents:

Would you believe you can prepare your child for sixth-grade math and science by one simple and fun activity in your home? When children cook, they have real-life experiences with concepts they will be taught later in the elementary years. It's easier to understand adding fractions when you've added ½ cup of sugar and ¼ cup of sugar rather than using a ¾ cup measure. The science concept of solids and liquids is more understandable when you've melted butter. And every child who has put cookies on a cookie tray knows that three times four equals 12 (which is also a dozen). Working in the kitchen teaches more than any page in a workbook ever did. Cooking gives your child a chance to internalize learning that is presented later in childhood, giving your child a great head start.

Start involving your child with small tasks such as chopping with dull, plastic knives and adding ingredients to a bowl. Move up to cracking eggs, rolling out dough, and shredding cheese. I cannot emphasize safety enough. Cooking with children can take extra time because it is necessary to be right next to your child, supervising every move. But the rewards of cooking are numerous and permanent.

Here is a beginning list of some ways you can make the most out of cooking with your child.

To reinforce science concepts:

- Teach your child to use all five senses while cooking.
- Talk about how heating and cooling changes foods.
- Identify ingredients as liquids or solids.
- Talk about differences in density of ingredients.

To reinforce math concepts:

- Let your child measure with cups and teaspoons.
- Compare the sizes of various ingredients.
- Count the number of seconds you mix something instead of using a timer.

To reinforce language concepts:

- Read the recipe together and talk about its sequence.
- Find new vocabulary words in the recipe.
- Have your child copy and mail the recipe to a relative.

To reinforce social studies concepts:

- Talk about what country or ethnic group the recipe comes from.
- Point out that you and your child are cooperating to meet a goal.

Sincerely,

Emotions and Learning

Dear Parents:

Emotions matter in our classroom. In my desire to educate the whole child, the area of emotional development is an important focus. Emotions have an impact on how each student learns in the classroom and the level of success he or she will experience in life. How people handle emotions has been referred to as emotional intelligence, which fortunately can be taught. Some skills associated with high emotional functioning are:

Self-awareness	Self-acceptance
Identifying emotions	Managing emotions
Empathy	Confidence
Self-motivation	Persistence
Assertiveness	Handling stress
Ability to communicate	Self-control
Cooperation	Curiosity
Personal responsibility	And many more

Emotions affect how students learn. Emotion drives attention. When a student's attention is focused on a task, that child is more likely to remember what he or she learned as a result. Lessons that are active in nature, such as role-playing, group projects, and physical activities, are ones that emotionally involve students and result in more information being stored in a student's memory. Emotional engagement leads to more permanent learning of concepts in the classroom.

By providing a risk-free atmosphere, my students are not subject to nonproductive stress that interferes with learning. Having a positive emotional climate in the classroom is an important ingredient in helping my students reach their potential.

Emotions affect how students live. IQ alone is not an accurate predictor of future success. Children with poor social relations are eight times as likely to drop out of school in later years than their emotionally intelligent counterparts. Emotional finesse is becoming increasingly more in demand in the workplace. Helping your child to develop emotional intelligence is as important as any academic work your child will do in school.

Sincerely,

Letter 8.6

Expectations

Dear Parents:

Behind every successful student is an adult who had high expectations for that child. Children mirror what adults think of them. Therefore, if you expect your child to be a good listener, for example, your child's skills in that area will develop. If you expect little from your child, you will get just that—little. Parents are the most important factor in a child's self-esteem, and having expectations that require a stretch, but are still within your child's grasp, contributes to feelings of self-worth when those expectations are met.

Expectations need to be high. Children truly will live up to what is expected of them. Communicate your expectations with a steady and confident voice to your child. You give your child wings by communicating your faith in him or her.

Expectations need to be reasonable. As adults, sometimes we forget what it's like to be a child. It might seem like we were adding three-digit numbers in first grade, but most of us were not. Read about developmental stages and what children at your child's age are typically able to do. If you have questions about setting appropriate academic expectations for your child, see me and we'll discuss your child's individual needs.

Examine your own biases. In subtle ways, we can communicate to a child myths such as math is for boys and girls read earlier. We might also remember a difficult school subject from our youth and project that dislike to a child. It is important also to avoid labeling. If a child hears over and over, "Tommy is the artistic one and Lucy is the math whiz," these roles become more firmly rooted, denying each child the opportunity to develop a well-rounded self.

Parents who have high expectations have been shown to monitor their children more closely, which is part of the charm of setting high standards. So deciding upon reasonable expectations, communicating them to your child, and monitoring your child's progress is a recipe for success.

Sincerely,

Integrated Curriculum

Dear Parents:

In our classroom, time is not set aside to study reading, and then later math, and maybe social studies after lunch. I combine these and other subjects for my students, a method that is called integrated instruction. While studying gardens, for example, we might set up a plant growth experiment (science), measure plant growth (math), keep an experiment journal (writing), find on a map where this plant is typically found (geography), and read books on gardening (reading). The same concepts and skills are taught as when the subjects are separated. The benefits of integrated instruction are:

- Students often don't see how school learning relates to real life. Integrating subject matter helps students see how the pieces of what they are learning fit together.
- Because the material presented is meaningful, it is more likely to be stored in long-term memory.
- Integrating subject areas is more time effective. More learning can take place when the day is not fragmented.
- Subjects are usually integrated around a theme. Themes allow students to study a subject in depth, such as "community helpers" or "rocks."
- Because themes are designed to spark my students' interests, they are highly motivational. When students become emotionally engaged in a topic, greater and more permanent learning takes place.

What is not meaningful, for children as well as adults, is usually forgotten. By using integrated instruction and themes, the chances are increased that your child will see school as relevant to real life and worth making an effort to succeed in.

Sincerely,

Learning Through Play

Dear Parents:

As a teacher, I have a vision of what kind of learners my students will be when they hit fifth grade. They will be self-directed with high degrees of initiative. They will be able to plan effectively and solve problems. My former students will take risks and learn more as a result. In short, their state reports will be works of art; their science fair projects will rival Nobel's best.

High-achieving fifth graders not only have figures and facts memorized but also have the above-mentioned behaviors that make them active, successful learners. These behaviors are learned in the early years through play. Play is a building block for your child's later school years, and its importance cannot be underestimated.

Through play, your child joins a distinguished club of children called "tinkerers." Famous past members of this club include the Wright brothers, Margaret Mead, and Thomas Edison, who were all encouraged to play as children. When children tinker, their hands are active. Active hands produce an adrenaline surge, which promotes greater learning. A child engaged in play is building habits of thinking that will carry forward in the years to come.

The social benefits of play are innumerable. Playing children learn to share, take turns, cooperate, show compassion, assert themselves, and exhibit patience, among other social skills. Play also provides a sense of accomplishment and allows children to feel success on a daily basis.

In addition to successful behaviors children learn through play, they also learn much about the world around them. Take, for example, just a smattering of what can be learned through one afternoon in the block area:

Hand/eye coordination	Balance and symmetry
Gravity	Size, shape, distance, proportion
Properties of matter	Counting
Classification	Sorting
Problem solving	Communication
Cause and effect	Fractions
Balance	Trial and error
Volume	And much, much more

So when your child's fifth-grade teacher is teaching about fulcrums and levers, your child can draw back on those days in the block corner and have a true understanding of what happens when you put the rectangle block on the triangle block. Play experiences for your child now are essential and truly educational.

Sincerely,

Multiple Intelligences

Dear Parents:

Can intelligence be summed up by a single IQ score? Not according to Howard Gardner, Professor of Education at Harvard and author of *Frames of Mind,* who believes there are a number of ways of being smart:

Linguistic intelligence. Students strong in this area have a capacity to use words effectively, both oral and written. Linguistic children love to play with words and often can be quite persuasive with them. They enjoy storytelling, word puzzles, and of course, reading and writing.

Logical-mathematical intelligence. Logical-mathematical thinkers feel for numbers what linguistics feel for words. They enjoy number games and are adept problem solvers. Logical-mathematical children prefer sequenced, orderly activities. They ask questions in a logical manner and their reasoning is solid.

Spatial intelligence. If your child has a lot of spatial intelligence, he or she responds to visual cues. The ability to see the world and graphically represent it in some form (as in a painting or a model) is a mark of spatial intelligence. Often, these children have a talent for art.

Bodily-kinesthetic intelligence. Most young children appear to be bodily-kinesthetic at first glance. This intelligence is marked by physical activity. Bodily-kinesthetic learners get more out of a lesson if they are moving while learning. Touching and feeling are important ways of gaining information for bodily-kinesthetic learners.

Musical intelligence. Children with musical intelligence thrive in an environment filled with rhythm and song. These children can memorize anything if put to a beat. They like listening to the sounds around them.

Interpersonal intelligence. Interpersonal intelligence involves the ability to "read" another person and respond appropriately. Students with this intelligence are social and often good leaders. These are the "street smart" kids.

Intrapersonal intelligence. Intrapersonal learners have a good understanding of who they are and why they behave as they do. They often are self-motivated. These children can be perceived as different, partially due to the fact that they like to spend time alone.

Sincerely,

Music and Learning

Dear Parents:

When you sang "Rock-a-Bye Baby" to your child as an infant, did you know you were preparing him or her for reading and math in school? You were, and you continue to do so every time you sing with or play music for your child. Not only is music good for your child's well-being, it is good for your child's brain.

Students who have studied music have been shown to have elevated SAT scores, and it's no coincidence. Here is how music enriches your child's growing brain:

- **Enhanced spatial reasoning.** Neural pathways in the cerebral cortex of the brain are strengthened by music, according to cognitive experts. This is where spatial reasoning occurs, which involves seeing the relationships between objects. Ordering notes and visualizing all the pieces that go into a song requires the same thought processes involved in geometry and solving puzzles.
- **Accelerated language development.** Learning music involves tuning in to differences in sounds, which is an important reading skill. Music and language both involve using symbols. Through singing, as in reading, children work with phrases and their meanings. Music exposes children to rhythm and rhyme, and is a natural companion to writing poetry.
- **Increased memory.** We could all sing the words to "I'm a Little Teapot" in unison. The music has imprinted that information in our brains. Melody and rhythm make for great memory aides.

Children are born with musical ability, which is lost if not used. Examine your home's musical environment and look for ways to bring it to life. You don't need to be musical yourself to share music with your child. A positive attitude toward music is all that's required. Some other ideas to get you started are:

- Make music with your child.
- Sing any directions you might need to give.
- Encourage your child to create musical instruments.
- Attend musical performances with your child.
- Share your musical favorites.
- Consider music lessons.

The positive effects of music are not just academic. Music can calm the cranky and relax the feisty. Music feeds our souls. It can be used to bring feelings to the surface. It spurs conversation and bonds us all together.

Sincerely,

Reading Aloud to Your Child

Dear Parents:

What is the most important thing you can do to ensure your child's school success? Read to your child on a daily basis. The National Commission on Reading found adults reading to children to be the most important factor in reading success. Reading aloud to children improves listening and language skills, stimulates imagination, expands understanding of the world, builds comprehension, and increases vocabulary.

Jim Trelease, author of the ever-popular *The Read Aloud Handbook,* says that "people are not illiterate as much as they are lazy, and they're lazy because they have no pleasure associations with reading." Create those associations with your child. The investment in reading aloud need not be great—15 minutes per day is all that's needed to reap these rewards. Carving out that time on a daily basis is the challenge. Regarding reading aloud as essential, not as a frill, is a good first step. Some strategies to help with read-aloud sessions are:

Preview the book. Talk about the title, author, and illustrator each time. Look at the cover and predict what the story might be about.

Read with expression! Your first- and second-grade teachers probably told you to do the same thing. Make the reading interesting by changing your voice to match the dialogue and adding emphasis where needed. Ham it up. A common mistake when reading, however, is to read too fast. Give your child time to visualize what you are reading.

Take time to talk. Ask questions that might have more than one answer to encourage thinking. Let your child ask questions, too. Draw your child's attention to details and help your child predict what might happen next in the story. Above all, follow your child's lead. He or she may not want to stop and talk at certain points.

Troubleshoot. If your child loses interest, take a break. Don't expect your child to "be quiet and listen" all the time. Find stories you and your child will both enjoy. Discontinue reading a book if it is obviously a poor choice. Don't start a read-aloud session if you don't have time to give it justice.

Make good choices. When an adult reads to a child at his or her own interest level, which may be beyond the child's reading level, it stretches the child's understanding and makes the child want to improve reading skills. Steer clear of books above your child's emotional level, however. Don't be afraid of reading a book over and over. A favorite book most likely appeals to your child's interest or emotional needs.

Read-aloud time is a perfect opportunity to slow down and show no sign of hurry. Your child will never forget the hours you spend together reading.

Sincerely,

On Child Development

Information on child development helps parents to set appropriate expectations for their children. The topics of these letters revolve around issues that follow the child's development throughout the early school years.

Rationale for
Sending Home These Letters

Conversation Letter. Conversation is a skill that children develop over time. Send home this letter to give parents tips on enhancing conversations with their child.

Dealing With Anger Letter. Children who can't handle anger effectively suffer. This letter lists tips to help end the suffering for kids who can't manage their anger.

Developmental Differences Letter. This letter puts development in perspective by offering stories of famous achievers who had lags in their development. Use this letter with parents who are anxious about their child's development.

Developmentally Appropriate Classroom Letter. Listed in this letter are descriptors of a developmentally appropriate classroom. Sending home this letter helps parents see the value in respecting each child's individual developmental timetable.

Fears Letter. Children in the early years have fears, some of which may interfere with school functioning. This letter gives tips for helping children conquer their fears.

Feelings Letter. Children who know how to express and deal with their feelings free themselves up to learn more in the classroom.

Giving Children Attention Letter. Some children do not receive adequate attention, others demand too much attention. Use this general letter on attention to address both problems.

Conversation

Dear Parents:

I hear far too many discussions in the classroom that go something like this:

Student 1: I went to dinner last night and saw Charles Barkley.
Student 2: Really? I saw Michael Jordan once at the mall.
Student 1: It was so great. When he sat down, he shook his napkin and his silverware fell on the floor.
Student 2: Oh, yeah? Michael Jordan gave my sister his autograph.

Another example of two kids chattering away, carrying on two monologues that don't add up to a dialogue. The art of conversation comes naturally to few students. Children need to be taught about the "give-and-take" of true communication.

Kid talk can be a one-way street, unless the following skills are taught:

Starting a conversation. Children need to look for cues that signal someone is ready to talk. They need to know how to approach the other person in a friendly way. Watching for the other's person's interest in the topic of conversation also is essential.

Active listening. One half of a good conversation is in the listening. Active listening involves looking at the speaker, freeing oneself of distractions, and showing receptive body language by keeping still and open to the speaker.

Asking questions. We all feel like we've been heard when people ask questions that are related to what we've said. Teach your child to pay attention to his or her curiosity during a conversation.

Ending a conversation. Instead of just dropping a topic, children need to explain if they need to leave a conversation. Before ending the conversation, the child should give the other person a chance to finish what he or she was saying, if possible.

Your conversations with your child are the best lessons for learning conversation skills. If it's hard to get your child to talk, consider using the following approaches:

- Ask open-ended questions (ones that require more than a one-word answer).
- Ask "What if . . . ?" questions to spark creative thinking.
- Notice something and wait for a response ("That car is a funny color").
- Ask "What was the best part of the day today?"

Sincerely,

Dealing With Anger

Dear Parents:

Anger is a natural part of life and is just one in a long list of feelings facing children and adults. Effective anger management is part of your child's emotional development, which makes it a concern in the classroom. Also, the ability to deal effectively with anger has been linked to higher math and reading scores, greater attention spans, and less behavioral problems in the classroom. Children who know how to deal with strong feelings such as anger can devote more of their energies toward learning.

Anger is often a sign of someone who feels powerless or out of control. At times, it can be a mask for other feelings, such as hurt, frustration, and embarrassment, among others. Teaching children to identify the feeling of anger when it crops up is an important first step to its management. Here are other ways to help children deal with anger:

- Teach your child the signs of anger. Noticing fists clenching or a racing heart can alert him or her to the signs of losing control.
- Help your child to identify things that make him or her angry, and teach your child how to deal with these causes before losing control.
- Show your child how to relieve tension associated with anger. Actions such as slow breathing and tensing and relaxing muscles help to reduce stress caused by anger and help a person regain control. Finding a distraction is another effective anger soother.
- Model for children how to express anger with words. Teach them a vocabulary for sharing feelings.
- Use and teach your child how to use "I-messages." I-messages allow people to express how they are feeling in an assertive way. An I-message a child might use is "I was embarrassed when you laughed at me when I fell."
- Acknowledge your child's anger. When we see anger displayed, our natural tendency as adults is to silence it for fear of intensifying it. We can actually help children more by acting as a sounding board.

Anger can be a positive force. It can drive us to make much needed changes and help us to get out of hurtful situations. The message to communicate to your child is that there is nothing wrong with being angry sometimes. How the anger is expressed is what really matters.

Sincerely,

Developmental Differences

Dear Parents:

Your child's developmental path will take many zigs and zags before your child reaches adulthood. There will be times of growth, times of stability, and yes, even times of regression. (When your child seems to regress in a certain area, look for marked growth in some other area.) Your child's developmental timetable is in part subject to factors beyond control, and some phases in your child's life need waiting out, while others will be most enjoyable. To illustrate the importance of giving each child the time and space he or she needs to grow, we can look at historical late bloomers:

> Thomas Edison, famous inventor of the electric light among other inventions, was considered mentally ill as a child and was told by his teachers that he couldn't learn.
>
> Louis Pasteur, the famous French scientist, received a grade of "mediocre" in chemistry at the Royal College.
>
> Louisa May Alcott, author of the classic *Little Women* and other famous novels, was told by an editor that she could never write anything that would sell.
>
> Leo Tolstoy, author of *War and Peace,* flunked out of college.
>
> Woodrow Wilson, former U.S. president, had difficulty with reading and writing. He learned to read much later than his age mates.
>
> Ludwig van Beethoven, the great composer, was called hopeless as a composer by one of his music teachers.
>
> Albert Einstein, the famous scientist, didn't learn to speak until four years of age or read until age seven. One teacher called him retarded.
>
> Abraham Lincoln, former U.S. president, went into the Black Hawk War as a captain and left as a private.
>
> Agatha Christie, the mystery writer, had trouble with spelling and writing as a child.
>
> Walt Disney, the cartoonist, was fired by a newspaper editor who said Disney had "no good ideas."

Development is characterized by peaks and valleys. After providing the best learning environment possible for your child, we can help your child by respecting his or her developmental timetable and by being patient through the valleys.

Sincerely,

Developmentally Appropriate Classroom

Dear Parents:

The education your child is receiving this year is developmentally appropriate, meaning that every attempt is made to match instruction and activities to my students' developmental levels. I use as a guide a 1987 publication by the National Association for the Education of Young Children, *Developmentally Appropriate Practice in Early Childhood Programs Serving Children From Birth Through Age 8,* which outlines effective teaching strategies and describes positive early childhood environments. The information in this document is based on over 30 years of theory, research, and practice in what works best in teaching young children. Characteristics of developmentally appropriate classrooms are:

- An emphasis is placed on educating the whole child in four domains: cognitive, physical, social, and emotional. All areas are seen as equally important.
- Children and teachers are encouraged to be lifelong learners.
- The children's interests are the basis for an integrated curriculum. Subjects like reading and math are not separated, because a young child's real life is not separated into subjects.
- Children acquire skills in reading and writing at their own pace.
- Good children's literature is readily available and is used in instruction.
- Children participate in making music, rhymes, and finger plays daily, and opportunities exist to create art with a variety of materials.
- Math understanding is developed through hands-on, concrete activities.
- Natural curiosity leads to science explorations.
- Attention is given to the development of large and small motor development.
- Play is respected as a learning activity.
- Choices are offered throughout the day.
- Self-esteem is enhanced and positive relations with classmates are fostered.
- Children think on higher levels.
- Parents are partners in their child's education.

Sincerely,

Fears

Dear Parents:

   Fears come and go throughout childhood, and they can pop up during times of new learning. Therefore, your child might have a resurgence of fears in the early school years. Fear is often about the unknown. Some fears we seem born with, such as the fear of falling, and others are learned through imitation or by experiencing a frightful event. Also, graphic warnings about taking precautions against some danger may cause fear in young children. Some fears are predictable, such as a fear of death, which often appears at around age five. Unfortunately, we can't take children's fear away, but we can help children learn to face and conquer fears. We can teach children that it's okay to be afraid, but that fear doesn't need to be paralyzing.
   If your child is struggling with some fears, here are ways you can help:

   Listen to your child's fears. Respect the reality of your child's fears by listening and clarifying the fear. Telling a child he or she doesn't need to be afraid is not helpful. Don't minimize the fear. In fact, do the closet and under-the-bed searches. Offer lots of reassurance. Point out to your child that you would never allow him or her to be in danger.

   Let your child know fears are normal. Assure your child that he or she is not the only one with a fear. Direct your child to remember other times when he or she faced fears and conquered them. Point to other people who have overcome fears, especially children at your child's age.

   Help your child handle the fear step by step. Breaking up fear-busting into small, manageable steps makes the process less overwhelming. If your child is afraid of the dark, start with leaving the hall lights on. Move up to a night light and then perhaps no light. Teach your child ways to distract himself or herself through the fear.

   Try to find the cause of the fear. Depending on the fear, there may be a basis for it. Fear can signal trouble. Therefore, certain fears should be investigated.

   Watch out for manipulation. Children sometimes use fear as a way of getting extra closeness and attention from a parent. If you suspect this with your child, look for ways to spend more time together when you can give your child positive attention.

   Check out a good book. Children's storybooks dealing with a variety of fears are plentiful. Sometimes a good book can be the turning point in letting go of a fear.

Sincerely,

Feelings

Dear Parents:

"How do you feel today?" If a child answers "I feel like I want to go home," that child is not recognizing his or her true feelings. This child could be feeling mad at a friend, hurt from being left out, or embarrassed by falling on the playground. The trouble is, until a feeling is recognized, it cannot be handled effectively. If the child said instead, "I feel sad because my block building fell down," I could guide the child to starting a new building, help him or her speak with the child who kicked over the building, or simply let the child unload the sadness. A child who recognizes an emotion and deals with it has freed himself or herself up for more learning in the classroom.

Identifying and expressing feelings takes practice. In addition, there are so many words that describe variations in feelings ("Are you feeling mad, irritated, annoyed, frustrated, furious?" None of these feelings is exactly the same). Helping your child build up a feelings vocabulary is a good first step. The way a person is feeling can usually be summed up in one feeling word. If your child lists a few feelings at once, help him or her zero in on the true feeling that overrides the rest of them.

Some children have formed the idea that there are good and bad feelings. This faulty thinking can interfere with managing feelings in a healthy way. We discuss in class how feelings are neither good nor bad—they just exist. What we do with our feelings can be positive or negative, but our actions are choices we make, whereas our feelings are not.

The children in our classroom are also taught to use "I-messages," which is a way of expressing feelings in an assertive way. The general formula for delivering an I-message is:

I feel _____ when you _____. I would prefer _____.

Example: "I feel angry when you kick over my block building. I would prefer you kick over just the buildings that you make."

I-messages help children become more self-aware and usually end in a peaceful resolution to a problem.

Listening to children's feelings can make adults want to jump in and give advice or fix things. Some adults are uncomfortable with extremes of emotions, and their first impulse is to quash the feelings that seem unpleasant. It takes patience to guide a child through his or her feelings without trying to control them. But as emotional coaches, it's our job to allow children to express emotions and help them find ways to deal with them effectively.

Sincerely,

Letter 9.7

Giving Children Attention

Dear Parents:

When your child needs more attention, you're probably well aware of it. Children sometimes misbehave to get attention they crave. If you feel annoyed, irritated, worried, or guilty in response to your child's misbehavior, these are cues that your child is begging for attention.

WAYS TO GIVE POSITIVE ATTENTION

- If your child has been waiting all day to spend time with you, invest 15 minutes before you take on cooking dinner or reading the paper. This time spent together benefits both of you.
- Set up a schedule for special time together, just you and your child, and stick to it.
- Give lots of hugs throughout the day.
- Set up a safe place where your child can play close by while you are cooking or paying bills.

HOW TO HANDLE BIDS FOR UNDUE ATTENTION

At times, some children feel they have to have a parent's constant attention. The parents of these children sometimes forget they have the right to some time to themselves. If you find yourself in this situation, you can:

- Brainstorm with your child healthy ways to get your attention.
- Redirect bids for attention by letting your child contribute in some way.
- Let your child see you spending time with other adults.
- If your child is interrupting excessively, let your child know you will ignore interruptions.
- Explain to your child that you understand his or her need for attention.

The trick is finding the balance: providing your child with enough healthy attention without giving in to every bid for attention. It's good also to remember that your child is only at this age once in his or her life, and attention given now transforms into wonderful memories in the future.

Sincerely,

PART III

Creating Letters for Behavioral Concerns

This section presents information to help with composing letters regarding behavioral concerns. The purpose of sending out these personalized letters is to inform parents of a problem with their child and to elicit their help. Often, problems that occur at school are also present at home. Therefore, parents are usually willing to support the teacher's efforts at home if asked. For your records, retain a copy of each letter you send. Staple the returned portion with the parent's signature to your copy.

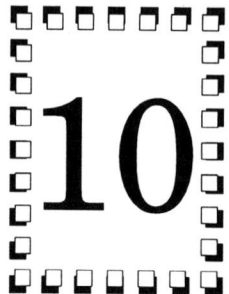

On Student Disrespect

When a student is disrespectful, it's best to act quickly and decisively. A good first step is to send home a letter describing the problem and offering suggestions for how home and school can work together. A letter sent home addressing disrespect is a profitable investment—the dividend will be a classroom based on mutual respect.

Sample Letter 10.1

Disrespect

(Letterhead)

Date

Dear (parent's name):

I have noticed (child's name) showing disrespectful behavior. (Child's name) has been disrespectful by (list as many situations possible where the child has been disrespectful:

Who: List if disrespect is toward students, teachers, and/or adults in the classroom.

What: Relate what the child actually has said or done.

Where: Tell if disrespect happens in the classroom, on the playground, and/or in the lunchroom.

When: Tell if disrespect occurs at a certain time of day or during certain activities.

Why: List any patterns to this behavior or anything that seems to trigger disrespect.)

So far, I have (list interventions used so far: communicated to the child in a kind but firm voice the unacceptability of disrespect, told the child about the importance of respecting each other, pointed out when the child responds respectfully). I suggest we focus in on this problem with your child for a week. When (child's name) responds respectfully, let's make an effort to direct (child's name)'s attention to these appropriate responses. In addition, we need to consistently deal with disrespectful behavior. A good first step is to use a consequence related to the disrespect. For example, if (child's name) reacts inappropriately when asking for something, that request should not be honored on the grounds of the disrespect. This is a good time to model our best respectful behavior and label it as such in front of (child's name).

I will be in touch with you after a week to review the effects of our working together to help (child's name) with this problem. I am confident that with our support, (child's name) will learn more acceptable ways to treat others. Please call me if you have any questions. Thank you.

Sincerely,

(your phone number)

- -

Please sign and return this portion of the letter by (date).

X_____
   Signature   Date

Sample Letter 10.2

Disrupting Group Time

(Letterhead)

Date

Dear (parent's name):

     I wanted you to know about a problem (child's name) is having with disrupting our group time.
     (List ways child is being disruptive:

     Who: Tell if the child disrupts when other children, the teacher, or classroom helpers are talking. Tell also if the child is being disruptive alone or with another child.
     What: Explain what the child does while being disruptive.
     Where: State if the child is disruptive on the rug, in his or her seat, or in some other place.
     When: Tell if the disruptions occur at a certain time of day or during certain activities.
     Why: Note any triggers to disruptive behavior.)

     I have (list interventions used so far: separated the child from distracting objects or children, reinforced appropriate group behavior, consistently communicated group procedures, removed the child from the group after giving a warning, looked for ways to give positive instead of negative attention). I recommend we both look for ways to notice the positive in (child's name), and make sure (child's name) is not enjoying negative attention. We can also set appropriate group behavior as a goal for (child's name).
     Learning how to work in a large group is a skill that sometimes needs extra encouragement. By both of us communicating the importance of following classroom procedures, I'm sure (child's name) will develop that skill. Thank you for your time. Please call me if you have any questions.

Sincerely,

(your phone number)

Please sign and return this portion of the letter by (date).

X_____
    Signature   Date

Sample Letter 10.3

Leaving Out Materials

(Letterhead)

Date

Dear (parent's name):

I have had to speak with (child's name) often about putting away (his or her) materials when finished with them.
(Describe the problem:

Who: Tell if the child leaves out materials in isolation or with a friend.

What: List what the child leaves out (math manipulatives, snacks, art supplies).

Where: Tell if the child leaves materials right where they were being used, or if they are partially put away. Does the problem occur more at his or her desk or at a learning center?

When: State the time of day this problem is most likely to occur.

Why: Tell if the child has difficulty ending an activity and runs out of time, or if the child prefers to be social during cleanup time.)

I have (list interventions used so far: reinforced when the child puts away materials, removed privileges associated with the materials when they are not picked up, paired the child with a responsible buddy). You can support our efforts at home by having the same expectations for picking up materials. Talk with (child's name) about the importance of being a contributing member of both the classroom and home. Set picking up materials as a goal for (child's name), and point out to (him or her) when (he or she) is successful with cleanup.

With home and school working together, I am sure (child's name) will learn to put away (his or her) materials in no time. Thanks for your help. Please call me if you have any questions.

Sincerely,

(your phone number)

- -

Please sign and return this portion of the letter by (date).

X_____

    Signature   Date

Sample Letter 10.4

Lying

(Letterhead)

Date

Dear (parent's name):

(Child's name) has had a problem recently with being dishonest.
(Describe the problem:

Who: Tell which child or teacher has been lied to.

What: Describe what the child has lied about.

Where: State where lying has taken place—in the classroom, on the playground, in special classes.

When: Tell if lying occurs more often during centers time, whole group sharing,
or some other consistent time.

Why: Describe situations that precede lying—show and tell, after a conflict with
a friend, to avoid getting in trouble.)

To help solve this problem, I have (list interventions used so far: modeled
truthfulness, reinforced honesty when observed, avoided questions that might lead to
lying). To encourage honesty, I suggest we (communicate unconditional positive
regard, teach that mistakes are a learning process, focus on solving problems when
they arise as opposed to blaming). Occasional lying is not uncommon in children—and
unfortunately in adults as well—but should be addressed so (child's name) can learn
better ways of coping.

If you would like to discuss this further, please do not hesitate to call. Thank
you for your time.

Sincerely,

(your phone number)

- -

Please sign and return this portion of the letter by (date).

X_____

    Signature   Date

Name Calling

(Letterhead)

Date

Dear (parent's name):

I am working with (child's name) on the problem of name calling. (Describe the problem:

Who: List which child has been insulted.

What: Describe any noticeable patterns to the content of the insults.

Where: Tell if the insults occur in the classroom, on the playground, or somewhere else.

When: Tell if the behavior occurs at a certain time of day.

Why: List any situations that prompt name calling.)

When (child's name) has called another child a name, I have (list interventions used so far: spoken with the child, reinforced positive interactions, asked the child to make amends, separated the child from whom he or she insulted). Please speak with (child's name) about other ways to handle anger besides name calling. Watch for name calling at home and discuss it with your child when it comes up. Reinforce when (child's name) is acting respectfully toward others.

Name calling is not uncommon at this age but needs to be stopped before it becomes a habit. Thanks so much for your time and attention to this matter. Please call me if you wish to discuss our efforts further.

Sincerely,

(your phone number)

Please sign and return this portion of the letter by (date).

X_____

    Signature   Date

Noncompliance

(Letterhead)

Date

Dear (parent's name):

I have been working with (child's name) on the problem of noncompliance. (Describe the problem:

Who: List which persons the child is noncompliant with, such as teachers, classroom assistants, parent helpers.

What: Describe the form of the noncompliant behavior, such as saying no, saying yes but not following through, walking away without responding.

Where: Tell if noncompliance occurs in the classroom, on the playground, or in some other setting.

When: Explain at what time of day or during which activities noncompliance is most likely to pop up.

Why: Describe situations that are likely to result in noncompliance, such as lining up, picking up materials, or joining the class for group time.)

When (child's name) has been noncompliant, I have (list interventions used so far: kindly but firmly repeated the request, reinforced compliance, removed privileges related to the noncompliance, ensured consistency in the classroom). You can support our efforts by emphasizing consistency and expectations at home. Reinforce appropriately compliant behavior. Compliance does not mean saying yes to everything, only to reasonable requests that are not harmful to your child. Helping (child's name) identify when to be compliant and when to say no is an important skill and one that may take a lot of practice.

Thank you for your time and support. Please call me if you wish to discuss this matter further.

Sincerely,

(your phone number)

_____

Please sign and return this portion of the letter by (date).

X_____

    Signature   Date

Nonparticipation

(Letterhead)

Date

Dear (parent's name):

(Child's name) has not been participating in some class activities.
(Describe the behavior:

Who: Tell if the child is skipping out on activities alone or with another child.

What: Describe what the child does instead of participating.

Where: List in what school settings the child is not participating, such as physical activities, activities involving getting messy, social activities, or academic activities.

When: State any time patterns to the nonparticipation.

Why: Tell what the child says about not wanting to participate, such as stating a dislike for the activity or showing shy behaviors.)

When (child's name) has been resistant to participate, I have (list interventions used so far: spoken to the child about why he or she should participate, led the child to the activity area in question, given step-by-step instructions on how to participate, withheld privileges associated with completing a task if that task was not completed, reinforced participation when observed). Please ask (child's name) the reason (he or she) does not participate at times and share these answers with me if helpful. Set participation in class activities as a goal for (child's name) and reinforce when (he or she) tells how (he or she) participated in class.

I think with a little encouragement from all of us, (child's name) will begin to participate more in class. Please call me if you would like to discuss this matter further. Thanks so much for your time.

Sincerely,

(your phone number)

Please sign and return this portion of the letter by (date).

X_____
    Signature   Date

Pouting

(Letterhead)

Date

Dear (parent's name):

I have noticed (child's name) is having a problem with pouting.
(Describe problem:

Who: Tell which person the pouting is directed to or which child it occurs with.

What: Describe what the pouting behavior looks like, such as long face, crossed arms, refusal to participate.

Where: List where the pouting occurs, such as in the classroom, in the lunchroom, at a certain learning center.

When: Explain what time of day pouting is most likely to occur.

Why: List situations that precipitate pouting, such as situations where the student is told no, free choice time, or structured time.)

When (child's name) pouts, I have (list interventions used so far: talked with the child when he or she is calm about the problem with pouting, ignored the behavior, redirected the child, reinforced cooperation, brainstormed alternatives to pouting, avoided power struggles). I suggest we both ensure that (child's name) does not prevail when pouting. Whenever possible, we can ignore any pouting behaviors and reinforce when (child's name) can express (his or her) feelings without pouting. We can point out and appreciate when (child's name) is able to pull out of a pout. In addition, we can temporarily avoid situations that might result in pouting to break the pattern of behavior.

Pouting is usually a fleeting behavior, but one that deserves attention lest it turn into a habitual means of coping. Thanks for your help with this problem. Let me know how (child's name) is progressing at home.

Sincerely,

(your phone number)

- -

Please sign and return this portion of the letter by (date).

X_____
    Signature   Date

Procrastination

(Letterhead)

Dear (parent's name):

(Child's name) has been having difficulty lately with procrastination. (Describe the problem:

Who: Tell which person is affected by the child's procrastination.

What: Tell what tasks the child has procrastinated in completing. Describe what the child does while procrastinating.

Where: State if the child procrastinates in the classroom, or in special classes such as art, music, or physical education.

When: State if procrastinating occurs more in the morning or afternoon, or during certain activities.

Why: Tell if you think the child is getting recognition or revenge (passively using power) by procrastinating, or if procrastination is a way to avoid work that seems difficult.)

When (child's name) procrastinates, I have (list interventions used so far: monitored and followed through on requests, set a timer for completing a task, reinforced on-task behavior). We both can help by monitoring (child's name)'s task completion and pointing out to (him or her) when a task is successfully completed. We can communicate our expectations that once a job has been started, it will be completed. We can also help by breaking down activities that may seem overwhelming into small, manageable steps.

Our attention to this problem now might prevent what could be a lifelong problem. Thank you for your attention to this matter. If you have any questions, please feel free to call me.

Sincerely,

(your phone number)

- -

Please sign and return this portion of the letter by (date).

X_____

Signature   Date

Sample Letter 10.10

Seeking Attention

(Letterhead)

Date

Dear (parent's name):

(Child's name) has been seeking attention in inappropriate ways.
(Describe the behavior:

Who: Tell which person the child has been seeking attention from.

What: Describe the attention-getting behaviors, such as interrupting, shouting in class, pestering friends.

Where: List the places where attention is sought, such as the classroom or the lunchroom.

When: Tell if attention seeking is greater in the morning or the afternoon.

Why: Give your opinion of why the child may be seeking attention, such as to feel like he or she belongs, because of a lack of social skills, out of craving attention from someone.)

When (child's name) is seeking attention inappropriately, I have (list interventions used so far: ignored the behavior, reinforced positive attention, used a nonverbal cue that means "I'll talk to you later," provided positive attention). Together, we can provide positive attention and make an effort to shoot a smile, a hug, or a wave your child's way every now and then to let (him or her) know we are thinking of (him or her). We can ignore bids for undue attention and reinforce appropriate attention-getting behaviors.

In time, (child's name) will realize that (he or she) doesn't need to have our attention all the time and will come to know other ways of belonging besides seeking undue attention. Please call me if you have any questions. Thank you very much for your time.

Sincerely,

(your phone number)

- -

Please sign and return this portion of the letter by (date).

X_____

    Signature   Date

Shouting in the Classroom

(Letterhead)

Date

Dear (parent's name):

(Child's name) is having a problem with shouting and making loud noises. (Describe the behavior:

Who: Tell which person the child is calling out to loudly. Mention if the shouting child has a "partner in crime."

What: State what the child is shouting or what kinds of noises are being made.

Where: Mention if the shouting is in the classroom, in the lunchroom, in the library, or somewhere else.

When: Tell if the shouting occurs more at a certain time of day.

Why: Describe situations that seem to stimulate shouting out or loud noises, such as circle time, centers, or silent reading.)

When (child's name) makes loud noises, I have (list interventions used so far: communicated classroom noise level expectations, ignored outbursts, separated the child from whole group gathering, reinforced appropriate voice levels). You can support our efforts at home by talking to (child's name) about using a voice level appropriate for indoors. It would be helpful if noise level expectations at home matched expectations at school, if they don't already. Notice when (child's name) is using an even voice and point it out to (him or her). If you think (child's name) uses a loud voice to get attention, ignoring the bids for attention may extinguish them. Tell (child's name) in advance that you will be doing this to help (him or her) break a bad habit.

I will be in touch with you after a week to let you know about (child's name)'s progress with this problem. If you need to speak with me further, please do not hesitate to call. Thank you.

Sincerely,

(your phone number)

- -

Please sign and return this portion of the letter by (date).

X_____
      Signature   Date

Swearing

(Letterhead)

Date

Dear (parent's name):

(Child's name) is having a problem with swearing.
(Describe the problem:

Who: List which person the child swears at or with.

What: Tell what the child said. Don't use the exact swear words, but describe them, such as a female dog, a part of the male genitalia. Keep in mind it's generally easier to write it in a letter than describe the word or words over the phone.

Where: Tell where the child is swearing. Is it on the playground when no adults are around, or is it in the classroom?

When: Tell the time of day in which the swearing occurred.

Why: Explain if the child was frustrated, trying to impress friends, or merely swearing casually.)

When I heard (child's name) swear, I (list interventions used so far: spoke with the child about the inappropriateness of swearing, asked the child to make amends to those offended by the swear word). Please reinforce my conversation with (child's name) by conveying the seriousness of using swear words at school. (Child's name) most likely doesn't know the real meaning of the swear word used and may be unaware of its effect. Look also for models in (child's name)'s life who might use swear words frequently. You might want to have a conversation with those people if (child's name) continues to swear.

With our guidance, this incident will most likely become a distant memory. If you need to speak with me about this further, please do not hesitate to call. Thank you for your time.

Sincerely,

(your phone number)

- -

Please sign and return this portion of the letter by (date).

X_____
    Signature   Date

Tattling

(Letterhead)

Date

Dear (parent's name):

(Child's name) is having a problem with tattling on (his or her) classmates. (Describe the problem:

Who: List which children the child routinely tattles on.

What: Describe the nature of the tattles, such as hitting, name calling, breaking classroom rules.

Where: Tell if the child tattles more on the playground, or in the classroom, in the housekeeping area, or in the block corner.

When: Examine if the tattling occurs at a consistent time of day.

Why: Tell if the child tattles for attention, out of an inability to solve problems, or for grown-ups to see the child as "the good one.")

When (child's name) tattles, I have (list interventions used so far: asked the child to explain why he or she is telling me, communicated my faith that the child can work out the problem, reflected the child's feelings, helped the child generate solutions he or she could try). You can support what we are doing at school by responding to tattling in a similar manner, if you are not doing so already. Encouraging (child's name) to solve (his or her) own problems, and giving (child's name) positive attention when (he or she) does, should cut down on the tattling.

Tattling is often a temporary phase, and with our help it could be an even shorter one for (child's name). Thanks so much for your time and support.

Sincerely,

(your phone number)

Please sign and return this portion of the letter by (date).

X_____

Signature   Date

Sample Letter 10.14

Temper Tantrums

(Letterhead)

Date

Dear (parent's name):

(Child's name) has been having temper tantrums at school.
(Describe the tantrums:

Who: Tell which person the child has tantrums in front of.

What: Describe what the child does, such as throws objects, kicks and screams, hurts others, breaks things.

Where: State if tantrums are more likely to occur in a certain part of the classroom or school.

When: Tell if tantrums occur at a consistent time of day.

Why: Explain what comes before most tantrums, such as social squabbles, cleanup time, being told no, being insulted.)

In response to (child's name)'s temper tantrums, I have (list interventions used so far: ignored the behavior, reinforced self-control, separated the child, helped the child come up with alternatives to tantrums). Please support our efforts at school by helping (child's name) discover other ways of expressing (his or her) feelings when upset. If we both refuse to give attention to (child's name) when (he or she) has tantrums, the temper tantrums will lose their reward. It's difficult to do, but it is probably the best way to stop this behavior. The key is to be consistent.

I would appreciate knowing what works for you when you see (child's name) having a tantrum. Our efforts together should help (child's name) lick this problem. If you need to speak with me, please don't hesitate to call. Thanks for your time.

Sincerely,

(your phone number)

- -

Please sign and return this portion of the letter by (date).

X_____
    Signature   Date

On Student Physical Violence

Matters of physical violence require that parents be on your side. Students might come home telling one side of the story, and these letters make sure parents see the whole picture. These letters don't seek to blame, but rather to enlist parental support in solving problems of physical violence in the classroom.

Aggression

(Letterhead)

Date

Dear (parent's name):

(Child's name) has been aggressive with (his or her) classmates.
(Describe aggressive behavior:

Who: List which person the child is being aggressive toward or with.

What: Describe the aggressive behaviors, such as hitting, biting, pushing, name-calling, destroying property.

Where: Tell if the aggression occurs more often on the playground, in the classroom, in the housekeeping area, in the block corner, or in some other area.

When: Tell if the aggression tends to happen at a certain time of day.

Why: State what the child says are the reasons for the aggression. Tell if you think the child does not know how to ask for what he or she wants, if there seems to be pent-up anger, or if the child is lacking in social skills.)

When (child's name) has been aggressive, I have (list interventions used so far: separated the child, spoken to the child about the inappropriate behavior, helped the child to list alternatives to aggression, asked if the child is angry about something). Please support our efforts at school by talking to (child's name) about (his or her) aggressive behavior. Try to pinpoint its causes. Look for pent-up anger your child might be holding. Look also at possible aggressive role models your child might have.

No matter how consistently and appropriately we react to (child's name)'s aggression, it may continue if the root causes of the aggression are not brought to light. I will communicate to you any information I uncover that would be helpful in working with (child's name). Please be in touch with me to tell me about progress (child's name) is making at home with this matter. Thank you for your time.

Sincerely,

(your phone number)

- -

Please sign and return this portion of the letter by (date).

X_____

    Signature   Date

Biting

(Letterhead)

Date

Dear (parent's name):

> (Child's name) bit a classmate today.
> (Describe the situation:
>
> Who: Name which classmate was bitten.
>
> What: Tell if the bite was in play, or an aggressive act. Tell where on the classmate's body the child bit.
>
> Where: Tell where at school the bite happened.
>
> When: Tell the time of day when the bite happened and during which activity it happened.
>
> Why: Tell what the child was trying to accomplish with the bite, such as attention, revenge, boredom relief, release of unpleasant feelings.)

When the bite happened, I (list interventions used so far: immediately separated the child, asked the child what he or she was feeling, brainstormed other ways to express feelings, directed the child to make amends). Please reinforce our efforts by speaking with (child's name) about this matter at home. If your child has a habit of biting at home, you might want to prevent biting before it occurs by looking for signs that precede a bite, reinforcing all positive ways of coping, and kindly but firmly communicating that biting is not acceptable.

If this should occur again, I will call you right away. Please call me if you have any questions or suggestions. Thanks for your time and attention to this matter.

Sincerely,

(your phone number)

Please sign and return this portion of the letter by (date).

X_____

Signature   Date

Destroying Work of Others

(Letterhead)

Date

Dear (parent's name):

We have been having trouble with (child's name) destroying (his or her) classmates work.
(Describe problem:

Who: Name whose work the child has destroyed.

What: Tell what the child has done, such as coloring on another child's paper, cutting or crumpling up someone else's work, knocking over block buildings.

Where: Tell if the destruction happens in a certain area in the classroom, such as the art center or the writing center.

When: State if the destructive behavior is more common at certain times of the day, such as in the afternoon, during handwriting practice, or in the middle of transitions.

Why: Describe the child's demeanor during this behavior, and tell if the child is seeking attention or destroying out of frustration.)

When (child's name) has destroyed the work of others, I have (list interventions used so far: separated the child, talked to him or her about respecting the work of others, directed the child to make any repairs possible). Please reinforce the concept of respecting the work of others at home. Help your child to find healthier ways to get the attention of a classmate, or to express strong feelings.

I will let you know if this continues to be a problem. With our combined focus, we should be able to help (child's name) learn to respect the work of others. Please call me if you have any questions. Thanks for your time and support.

Sincerely,

(your phone number)

Please sign and return this portion of the letter by (date).

X_____
    Signature   Date

Sample Letter 11.4

Fighting With Friends

(Letterhead)

Date

Dear (parent's name):

(Child's name) has been involved in a number of fights with friends recently. (List the nature of the fights:

Who: Name which person the child is having difficulties with.

What: Explain your view of what the fights seem to be about.

Where: Tell if the fights occur in the classroom, on the playground, in the lunchroom, or in special classes.

When: Describe the time of day or during which activities the fights usually occur.

Why: Tell what is triggering the fights.)

I have (list interventions used so far: mediated between fighting parties, separated children from each other and from certain activities, reinforced friendly behaviors). You may want to talk about these friendship problems at home with (child's name). Make a list of ideas for coping when a fight looks possible. Help your child to see (his or her) responsibility in the disputes, also. Share stories of how you dealt with fighting as a child. Above all, listen.

By focusing our collective attention on this problem, I believe we can help (child's name) deal with these friendship trials. Thank you for your time and attention. Please call me if you wish to discuss this matter further.

Sincerely,

(your phone number)

Please sign and return this portion of the letter by (date).

X_____

Signature   Date

Hitting

(Letterhead)

Date

Dear (parent's name):

(Child's name) has been having a problem with hitting other students.
(Describe the problem:

Who: Name which classmate the child has been hitting.
What: Tell if it is aggressive hitting or hitting meant to be fun.
Where: State if the hitting is taking place in the classroom, on the playground, or somewhere else.
When: Tell at what time of day the hitting usually occurs.
Why: Explain if the child hits out of frustration, to defend property, to get his or her own way, or to get attention.)

When (child's name) has hit another child, I have (list interventions used so far: separated the child, spoken with the child about appropriate ways to express strong feelings, guided the child to make amends, helped the child to make a list of alternatives to hitting). Please speak with (child's name) about this problem, and brainstorm together better ways of coping. We have a zero tolerance for hitting in the classroom, which you may want to extend at home, if you aren't already. The key is to respond firmly (while still being respectful) if (child's name) hits someone.

We have a rule in the classroom: "Never hurt anyone on the inside or the outside." Referring (child's name) back to that rule should cut down on some of the hitting. Please don't hesitate to call if you have any questions or would like to discuss this problem. Thank you very much for your time and attention to this matter.

Sincerely,

(your phone number)

- -

Please sign and return this portion of the letter by (date).

X_____
　Signature　　　　　　　　　　　　　　　Date

Property Destruction

(Letterhead)

Date

Dear (parent's name):

(Child's name) has been destroying some of our school materials.
(Describe problem:

Who: Tell if the child is working alone or with a partner.

What: List what the child is doing, such as coloring on tables or writing on walls, breaking game pieces, snapping pencils or crayons in two, or picking at bulletin boards.

Where: State if destruction occurs in the classroom, the lunchroom, or in special classes.

When: Tell if property destruction occurs at a regular time of day or during a certain activity.

Why: Tell what feelings are being displayed while destroying property, such as anger, boredom, clowning around.)

When I have noticed (child's name) destroying property, I have (list interventions used so far: asked the child to fix what he or she broke, spoken to the child about the importance of taking care of materials, asked the child what he or she was feeling at the time, removed the child from situations where destruction was a possibility). Please support our efforts by speaking with (child's name) about taking care of our classroom materials. Encourage this at home with (child's name)'s personal possessions, if you are not doing so already. Point out when your child is taking extra care with (his or her) things.

I will let you know if this problem continues. I hope, with our combined attention to this matter, (child's name) will begin to take better care of materials. Please call if you wish to speak about this further. Thank you for your time.

Sincerely,

(your phone number)

Please sign and return this portion of the letter by (date).

X_____

    Signature   Date

Stealing

[Note: This letter represents a problem that is more serious in nature and requires a verbal contact with parents. The purpose of this letter is to let the parent know the basics of what went on. Reading the letter before you talk with parents gives them the chance to digest the situation and talk it over with their child.]

(Letterhead)

Date

Dear (parent's name):

    I am writing this note to let you know that (child's name) took something that belongs to someone else.
    (Describe problem:)

    Who: Tell which person the child took the object from.
    What: State what the stolen object was.
    Where: Tell where the theft took place.
    When: Tell what time the theft happened. Estimate if you don't know.
    Why: State any reasons the child may have given for stealing.)

    In the early years, the desire to have an object that belongs to another child might make fuzzy the lines of ownership. Our job right now is to communicate that stealing is wrong without coming down too hard on (child's name), because this is the first time it has occurred. We need to explain that some desires are not attainable and talk to (child's name) about the concept of ownership.
    I will call you to discuss this matter further, but I wanted you to have a chance to speak with (child's name) before we talk. With our guidance, this will likely be the last time (child's name) takes something that doesn't belong to (him or her). Thank you for your time, and I'll talk with you soon.

Sincerely,

(your phone number)

- -

Please sign and return this portion of the letter by (date).

X_____
    Signature   Date

Throwing Objects at Others

(Letterhead)

Date

Dear (parent's names):

(Child's name) has had a problem with throwing things.
(Describe the problem:

Who: State if the child is throwing objects at a particular person.
What: List the objects the child is throwing.
Where: Describe in what setting the throwing occurs, such as in the classroom, in the lunchroom, on the playground.
When: Note if throwing objects follows any time pattern.
Why: Tell if the child is throwing out of anger, frustration, to get attention, to be mischievous.)

When (child's name) has thrown something in the classroom, I have (list interventions used so far: separated the child, spoken with the child about the danger of throwing objects, talked about feelings that came before throwing, helped the child list other ways to express emotion or get attention). Please help at home by communicating the seriousness of throwing objects in class. Set a goal with your child of finding other ways to react when angry, frustrated, hurt, or bored or when needing attention.

I will keep you posted on (child's name)'s progress in solving this problem. With all of us focusing attention on this problem, we should be able to help (child's name) eliminate throwing objects as a way of responding to stress. Please call me if you have any questions. Thanks for your time and support.

Sincerely,

(your phone number)

- -

Please sign and return this portion of the letter by (date).

X_____

Signature   Date

PART IV

Other Ready-to-Use Communication Forms

This section includes 20 ready-to-use resources for everyday classroom use. These forms can be sent home by adding just a few words to get your point across. *Reminders* can be sent home when you just need to be certain parents are remembering information, such as a conference time or an early release day. *Reports* give information on classroom happenings. *Requests* let you quickly send home pleas for materials or volunteers. *Surveys* help you know more about your parent community.

Conference Confirmation

Our conference to discuss _____'s progress is scheduled for_____. Please come with goal-setting ideas and any questions you might have. I'm looking forward to meeting with you. Thank you.

Sincerely,

Early Release Day

This is just a reminder that

_____

is an early release day. The students will be dismissed at _____.

_____ *did not bring*

lunch money or a lunch from home today.

Thank you for your attention to this matter.

Sincerely,

Just a reminder . . .

I am sending this note to remind you that . . .

Thank you for your time.
Sincerely,

Just a reminder . . .

There will be no school on

_____

Enjoy the day off!

Overdue Book

_____has a book from our school
library that is overdue. The book's title is

_____

Please look for the book at home and return it with your
child as soon as possible. If you can't locate this book,
please give me a call. Thank you for your time.

Sincerely,

Name_____ Date_____

Classroom Daily Behavior Report

1	**2**	**3**	**4**	**5**
Excellent behavior!	Good behavior, with perhaps one incident	Average classroom behavior, with some disruptions	Needed redirection often	Severe misbehavior

Comments:

Please sign and return this form. X_____

Ouch!

Date_____

_____ got hurt at school today. This is what happened:

I just thought you should know. Please call me if you have any questions. Thank you!
Sincerely,

Date_____

_____

did a great job of reading to our class today!

Your child
* **read with expression**   * **read loudly and clearly**
* **showed the pictures**   * **answered questions**
* **and in general was a wonderful classroom reader!**

Sincerely,

What an Accomplishment!

_____

has accomplished

_____

Date _____

Great work! Wow! Congratulations! Super!

Date_____ ***Call Me!***

*I need to speak with you about*_____

_____.

Please call me today at _____ *between the hours of* _____.

Thank you!

Sincerely,

Field Trip Permission Slip

Our class is going on a field trip. The details are:

Where_____

Date_____

Time of departure_____   **Time of return**_____

Who is going_____

What your child will need:

Please sign and return this permission slip.
I give my child permission to attend this field trip.

X_____
    Signature   Date

Name _____ Week of _____

Home Reading Log

Day of the Week	Title of Book (s)	Parent's Initials
Monday		
Tuesday		
Wednesday		
Thursday		
Friday		

Please return this form each Monday after it is completed. Thank you.

Form 14

I tried to reach you by e-mail.

From_____ E-mail address_____

Date_____ Time_____

Message_____

_____

_____

_____

Please sign and return this form. X_____

Form 15

I tried to reach you by phone.

From_____ Phone number_____

Date_____ Time_____

Message_____

_____

_____

_____

Please sign and return this form. X_____

We Are Cooking . . .

and we need your help! Your child has volunteered to bring in the following ingredient:

_____

Please send in the ingredient by _____, and call me at _____ if you are unable to help at this time. Thank you!

Sincerely,

We need . . .

We are working on a project and are looking for donations of the following:

If you can help us, please send in your contribution by _____.
Thank you!

Sincerely,

Volunteer Calendar

Parent's name_____ Month of _____

M	T	W	Th	F

Please sign up to help in our classroom. Please write your name in the date square or squares to indicate when you would like to come in. Thank you for continuing to be a partner in your child's education.

If you can't come in to help, but would still like to contribute to our classroom, please call me for suggestions on ways you can help at home.

Parent Interest Survey

Sharing your interests, hobbies, talents, and occupations with your child's class will make our room a richer place this school year. Please indicate below how you can share yourself in our classroom this year.

Helping in the Classroom

      room parent _____
      classroom volunteer _____
      classroom reader _____
      art projects _____

Helping at Home

      cutting, stapling,
      assembling projects _____
      special-event baker _____
      book-order parent _____
      library runner _____

List hobbies (such as collecting stamps, gardening) you could share with our class:

Would you be willing to speak to our class about your occupation? If so, describe below:

_____

Your name   **Date**

Thank You!

What Are Your Expectations?

As partners in your child's education, it is important for us to be aware of each other's values regarding what your child should be learning this year. I will communicate my beliefs at back-to-school night. Please take a moment to jot down what your expectations are of me this year, and what you hope your child will learn. (For example, if you are an advocate of using children's literature, learning basic math facts, or lots of homework, let me know.) This will begin a dialogue between us that will continue throughout the year. Please return this form to me as soon as possible. Thank you for your time and for being a partner in your child's education.

Sincerely,

Child's Name _____

My expectations for this year are . . .

_____
Signature   *Date*

Please continue on the back side of this form or attach another page if necessary.

Bibliography

Bredekamp, S. (Ed.). (1987). *Developmentally appropriate practice in early childhood programs serving children from birth through age 8.* Washington, DC: National Association for the Education of Young Children.

Gardner, H. (1985). *Frames of mind.* New York: Basic Books.

Glauber, A., Nichols, V., & Watts, V. M. (1983). *Basic skills in the U.S. workforce.* New York: Center for Public Resources.

McGinnis, E., & Goldstein, A. P. (1984). *Skillstreaming the elementary school child: A guide for teaching prosocial skills.* Champaign, IL: Research Press Company.

Nelson, J. (1996). *Positive discipline.* New York: Ballantine.

Trelease, J. (1995). *The read aloud handbook.* New York: Penguin.